A WOODSMAN REMEMBERS

The Life and Times
of
James D. Anderson

James D. Anderson - 1942

*To the memory of my wife,
Marie, who filled my life
with love for 59 years.*

Marie Hobson Anderson
1915-1996

INTRODUCTION

My name is James Anderson, I am eighty years old and this is an introduction to the stories I am going to tell you.

I was born during World War I which ended when I was about two years old. The first thing I remember when I was a little boy were the train whistles blowing when the war ended.

When I was about four years old we were living in North Bellingham in the Eureka District. We lived there until my dad bought a place on Lake Samish and built a chicken farm. He built three great big chicken houses – one was twenty feet wide and eighty feet long and two of them were twenty feet wide and forty feet long. My father had one chicken house made into a brooder house where he put incubators for eggs so he could raise chickens. He raised about 6,000 chickens a year. Part of them would be laying hens and part of them would be roosters etc.

My dad was a heavy drinker – he worked hard and he drank hard. He was hard to get along with. We lived there on the Samish Road until I was about seventeen years old. While living there and going to school, I became very interested in the Boy Scouts, but as I was only ten years old they wouldn't let me join. Mama said I had to wait until I was a little older. So I waited until I was twelve and although I was still a little young I joined Boy Scout Troop No. 27. In those days you had to be voted into the Troop, you couldn't just join. You had to learn the Scout Oath and the Scout Law before they would let you join. I remember being in Troop 27 where we had three patrols with eight boys in each patrol. I liked it very much and that was where I learned to make a lot of friends.

I learned a lot of things in the Boy Scouts, but I didn't do very well in school until I was in the seventh grade. My mother and family couldn't cut my hair and I had long hair and the teachers made fun of me and would put ribbons in my hair and stand me up in front of the class. The other kids didn't think I was very smart and didn't like me at all. I finally grew out of that and when I got into the sixth, seventh and eighth grades we had a principal by the name of Mrs. Workman who thought a lot of me. She did a lot for my education (what little education I had) and the kids liked me and I did pretty well in school and in the Boy Scouts.

My dad left home when I was fourteen and I had to go out and go to work for a living, cutting pulp wood and work like that. There were four of us boys left at home and we all had to go out to work and provide with what we could get. We always had plenty of food, but clothing was a problem as we never had much money for clothes. If you had ten cents you were lucky.

Chapter 1

When I was seventeen years old I was out of school. My older brother, Jess, worked down at Sumas on a big farm. I remember the old farmer's name was "Meer". Jess had to go somewhere so he couldn't stay out there, and farmer Meer was hard up for somebody to work for him. Mom asked if I would go out and help old man Meer hay, and I asked, "How much am I going to get paid for it?" She said, "Nothing, if you just get your room and board you'll be lucky." I had only ten cents in my pocket when I started hitchhiking. I got out as far as a place called Lawrence and I was hungry, so I bought a quart of buttermilk. That was really something! I hiked out to Meer's farm which was a good one. He had about 18 or 20 cows to milk and he had to get the haying done. My job was to harness the team of horses to the mowing machine and mow the hay. After the hay was mowed I would get a rake and rake it all up in rolls so it would dry and then we would put it on the wagon and haul it into the barn.

One day while I was mowing I hit a yellow jacket's nest and the yellow jackets hit the horses and the horses ran away. I had a hard time stopping them, but finally got them stopped up against a fence. I just kept on haying and when I got back to the barn the old man asked, "Jimmy, what were you running those horses for?" I said, "I wasn't running them – the yellow jackets were running them – the yellow jackets had chased them down there." I handled that all right and after a few days I got the haying all done. Then I raked the hay and put it in rolls so it would dry and the old man and I went down and shocked it.

I don't know if you know what shocking is, but you take a pitchfork full of hay and you put it in big high shocks, then you take a wagon built with a hayrack on it which one person drives while four or five people put the hay on the wagon. You had to pile it up just so. When you get to the barn you have what you call a hayfork that will go up and hit a trolley and go back in the barn and somebody will be up in the barn and pull a rope and trip the hay.

Sometimes there will be half a ton of hay on one fork. You wouldn't believe it unless you saw it – it was quite an operation. In the barn there was a quarter inch cable hooked up to that thing because it would get pretty heavy. While we were hauling in the hay I always pulled the wagon up to the hay barn where the big door was so the old man could get up and hook the fork in the hay. Then I would have to unhook the team and go around and put it on what was called a straw line (a straw line is a quarter inch cable hooked to that hayfork) and pull it up to the trolley where it would go back into the barn and it had a rope on it that the guy in the barn would pull to trip the hay. There would also have to be someone in the barn on the hayrack to put the fork in the hay.

One day the old man, Meer, was up on the hayrack where he had just gotten that hayfork into the hay. I hooked the team up to the straw line and picked up the reins which had dropped out of my hands onto the ground. There was usually a lot of horse manure on the ground and a lot of yellow jackets around. When I picked up the reins there was a yellow jacket on them which I grabbed and pinched, and that scared the heck out of me. I let out a yell that scared the horses and started them running from me just as the old man had that hayfork into the hay. When they started running away with it they threw the old man way out into the manure pile and the thing went up in the hayrack and that fork went way up into the barn and snapped back. If it had not been for a stopper the barn would have been pulled over.

I had an awful time stopping those horses because they just ran completely wild when my scream scared them. I quieted them down and brought them back. The old man was so mad at me that he said he ought to send me home. I told him that I would be glad to go home, but Mom had told me to help him. He asked, "What did you do that for?" I had to explain to him that the reason I let out that yell was because a yellow jacket had stung my finger.

He told me, "You had better go up in the barn and see what happened to old John." Old John, who was ninety-five years old , was his wife's brother and a very religious old fellow. Meer said, "You go up and see what happened to old John, because he could have gotten covered up with hay and you might have to look for him."

When I got up in the hay loft I hollered for John and heard him

10

way down in the hay pile. I said, "John, how are you?" He said, "I'm O.K." I said, "Wait a minute and I'll get a pitchfork and get the hay off of you." He started yelling because he was afraid I'd hit him with the pitchfork. It took awhile to dig him out of the hay and when I finally got to him I said, "What did you think went wrong, John?" He answered, "I thought the Devil had hold of me and I was a gonner." I said, "Well you're O.K. now aren't you?" To which he replied, "Yeah." "Boy, look at my watch," he said, as he pulled out a big gold watch and looked at it. I liked the old man because he had a good sense of humor.

Chapter II

When I was about seventeen years old my Mother, my three brothers and I moved to Mt. Vernon, Washington . . . that is southwest of there in a place called Avon where we went to work for my Uncle Jim.

My oldest brother was a teamster and he had a team of horses to work on the farm. My brother, Alec, and I worked in Golden Seal — hoeing and weeding. That was the first time anyone taught me how to work. At first my Uncle said I was just playing and if it hadn't been for his being my Uncle he would have "canned" me and sent me home. But he taught me the right way to work and we got a dollar and eighty cents per day, for nine hours work. We worked there for five or six months. I earned enough money to buy some good clothes so I could go to church, and that is where I met Marie Hobson, my future wife.

Marie & Jimmy
1934

The family left Avon that fall and moved back to Bellingham for some reason I can't remember. My Mother had to move back and we moved into my grand-father's old home place. When I was seventeen or eighteen years old the Depression was on, work was hard to get, and if you had a dime you thought you were rich.

My brothers, cousins and friends got a job cutting pulpwood out at a place called Wildcat Cove on Chuckanut Drive. The pulp mill would give us a dollar a cord for the pulpwood, and if you worked hard all day you could cut a cord of pulp. In those days you had to use a cross-cut saw to cut pulpwood. It had to be cut in logs about 4 ft. long and then you had to take an axe and peel 'em, then cut the black knots out of them. The pulp mill sent us over a couple of scows, which were more or less big rafts, that we could tie up to the shore. Each scow would hold about forty cords of pulpwood. We made a flume from the top of a hill that we would push the pulpwood into so it would go down and hit the scow. Somebody would have to go down there and pile it up.

I didn't cut pulpwood, but they had me drive an old mule and haul the wood on the skids on a sled. We built what you might call a little skid road down to the flume. The old mule seemed to be a pretty mean one and she would snap at me when I wasn't watching. I had the mule trained so that she would go on her own up the skid road to the cutters where they could load the pulpwood. By the time I got there they would have the sled loaded and I would have to get the thing turned around and start out again. I'd go ahead of the mule and put grease on the skid, which was about four feet apart and then the sled would pull easily on it.

I remember one time the mule reached over and bit me right in the backside. I got so mad I took a chunk of wood and hit her alongside the head and knocked her down. From then on "Old Babe" didn't snap at me any more. That is, she still snapped at me, but held her head way back. I remember the mule because I had to get up early in the morning and harness her, drive her about six miles to work, and then work all day with her.

One time when we had all the pulpwood on one of the scows a big storm came up and tore it loose. We had pulpwood scattered all over Chuckanut Bay and we couldn't get it all picked up. I remember my brothers and the others thought they had paid me a whole lot when they paid me one dollar for a week's work because they had lost so much money on it. Those were rough times!

Chapter III

[I]n November, 1934 I went into the C.C.C. (Civilian Conservation Corps). The Army maintained the discipline and the Forest Service had the work to be done. The Army could keep 25% of the men in camp and the Forest Service used the rest. I hadn't been there very long when a Lt. and the Forest Service lined us all up (there were about 200 men in camp) and asked who wanted to be surveyors or engineers. Though we scarcely knew what a surveyor or engineer was, two of us stepped forward. I remember the other boy turned to me and asked, "What's a surveyor?" Anyway, we were going to learn to be that.

The State Department of Natural Resources was the Forest Service that was helping the boys and that I worked for. We worked on old railroad grades, re-surveying them. They taught me how to use an Adney, which is an instrument for taking topog or taking average slope

Survey Team - 1930's

on both sides of the old railroad. We would also walk along and measure where the new culverts needed to be put in. We would take compasses and traverse it. Traversing your chain, you'd go so far and then change your angle and read your compass and then measure the distance. We did that for the entire winter.

One day as we were walking across a little log a young bear cub came out from under the log. He saw us and took off for the brush. I thought it would be a big deal to take him back to camp and so I started off after the little bear, but I couldn't catch him. Back in camp that evening I told the boys about the bear and they went up to catch it, but had no luck either.

About two days later some of the boys in camp talked the Lieutenant into taking them down to Sedro-Woolley to see a show. There was a Marshall down there whose name was "Handlebar Hank" who didn't like CCC boys. Some of the CCC boys sneaked out of the show and got "Handlebar Hank" to chase them down the railroad track to where they had a flour barrel ready to stuff him into. They stuffed him into the barrel, nailed a cross on it and dumped him over the bank. Some of us didn't know anything about it. The next day

*C.C.C. Camp,
Lyman,
Washington
November
1934*

the Sheriff, the Marshall, the State Patrol, the Lieutenant, and every officer you could think of lined us all up to find out who had done this. At first no one would tell, so they held us all in camp for over a month for not telling.

I remember every Friday and Saturday night in the CCC's the Lieutenant would get two Army trucks and take all the boys who wanted to go to see a show in to Sedro-Woolley. Sometimes there would be two truckloads and sometimes three. Each truck would hold about 22 boys. One Friday night they all went down there and there were always a bunch of rowdies a little bit rougher than the rest who would come out of the show looking for some whiskey.

They found some whiskey and then went looking for "Handlebar Hank". And they found "Handlebar Hank."They knew that a local law officer was not allowed to touch an Army truck to discipline CCC boys, and so they got the Marshall to chase them right to the back of an Army truck where they jumped in just as the Lieutenant got out of the movie and to the truck.

Chapter IV

We were in the CCC camp at Lyman during the summer of 1935. I remember that we had a lot of fires in the valley that summer. It seemed as though someone was lighting them. These were tough times and many local people didn't have jobs. It was suspected that they thought if they could get some fires started that they would get jobs fighting them. But what they didn't know was that was what the CCC boys were there for.

I remember fighting fires all that summer of '35. I remember putting a sandwich in my pocket and starting down a hill, slipping on a log and knocking myself out and Harry Osborn dragging me off from the fire.

One time the Lieutenant walked in and said to us, "You've got nothing to complain about, you're getting $25.00 per month to send home to your family and you're getting $5.00 a month for yourself. You're getting all of your clothes and all of your food and everything. Besides the $30.00 you're getting, it costs $80 a month to keep you boys, so you are not in bad shape at all for these times." I wanted to set that straight.

One Saturday nine boys hitchhiked from Lyman to Sedro-Woolley (about 9 miles) to get some whiskey. Somehow they got hold of some moonshine and when they returned to camp that evening they were so sick – so sick that they had to call in the doctors. The doctors weren't sure what to do for moonshine poisoning, but there must have been rubbing alcohol or something in it. Anyway those boys ended up at Fort Lewis and were there almost a month before they were released.

As I was saying, we were in camp in Lyman in 1934 and 1935 where I fought fern and brush fires. There were a lot of those fires in July and August because everything was so dry all through the old logging works in there. Some of the fires were started by the loggers and others by people who were out of work. The CCC boys must have put a lot of people out of work. We fought fires so much for two or three months that we were completely exhausted.

We stayed in that area until the fall and I worked with the engineers doing surveys and laying out roads, etc. That winter, probably in November, our camp was moved up to Index above Skykomish about 40 miles east of Everett. I remember it was pouring down rain while they were loading up the kitchen gear and I remember the cook singing "Hard Times" as we moved up into a brand new campground.

The old campground that we left was taken over by kids out of New York and I remember their asking about all the animals in the woods. They had come directly from the big city and some of them had never seen a tree and had the impression that there were wild Indians out here and bears and tigers and lions. They had the wildest imaginations because they hadn't been told the truth about what was really here.

We moved to Index about November, but the camp wasn't quite complete. The Lieutenant, who knew I had worked with the surveyors, came out and handed me a transit and told me to lay out some of the curves around the buildings. I said I didn't know anything about running a transit as all I had ever run was a compass. He said I had better learn, and that the best way for me to do that was to go right into the Education Building and see the Educational Supervisor whose name was Duncan.

The Educational Supervisor got me some books on angles and things, and how to use a transit. I learned sines and co-sines, tangents and co-tangents and latitudes and departures and all different formulas for figuring out curves. I must have spent two or three months there working on that deal and then I was shipped up to Skykomish to work with a couple of junior foresters, one of whom was named Roger and the other Paul.

There was a world of difference in their make-up. Roger was a wild person – I mean wild to a point. He liked to go to parties on Saturday night and raise heck and all that even though he had just gotten married. Paul had been married and was a quiet sort of a person. They were always ribbing each other about Friday and Saturday nights. I don't think they were over 24 or 25 years old.

Well, I remember we were way up behind Index and I had a compass and a staff – a staff being something you jab in the ground that has a ball bearing kind of rig on top of it that you set your compass on to level it and take a shot on up ahead. You set your eye on a point and walk on up to that point with a fellow behind you, and you drag a chain (that is a tape) and measure the ground. Usually that chain is a 200 ft. chain or tape, and when you come to the end of it the fellow will stop and holler "chain". At this point you stop and take another shot at it.

I remember one time I was walking down into the canyon of a creek bed where I took my staff and jabbed it into the ground . . . it didn't stop. That surprised me! Then I began to realize that I was above a shed that had been built over the creek, and that I had just discovered a moonshine still. It must have been that the people who ran it knew that we were working in the area and so they moved out and left it, along with two empty barrels. They probably figured on moving back when we were done.

In the CCC's we didn't have restrooms and bathrooms like they have nowadays. We had what they called an outside toilet. The outside toilet that was built for the CCC's was about four feet wide and 15 feet long and would have about eight or 10 holes in it. Eight or ten people could go in and use it at the same time. There were also showers in another building, but the toilet was a different setup. Under the seats was a trough with water running through it so that the waste could drop down into the trough and go out.

However to back up on my story, I had a car which my mother had let me buy. It was an old Chevrolet that I hadn't paid much for. I bought it so I could go to see Marie in Avon. The CCC boys weren't supposed to have cars, but I had this car hid over in the brush along with a whole lot of other cars the CCC boys had so they could take off on Friday nights. This particular Friday night happened to be the day before Christmas and we were going to get several days off. There were a couple other fellows who were going to ride with me.

That afternoon while I was taking a shower some kids were playing around in there and I ended up slipping and hitting my head on the concrete, and knocking myself out so I ended up in the infirmary. There was another fellow in there who was mad because he couldn't go home for Christmas. I told him, "Well, I'm going to get dressed and go home." The fellow worked in the kitchen and had eaten some shredded coconut that didn't digest and had gone right on through him. So he was sitting on the toilet there and the stool hit the trough and filtered on down. While he was there the Lt. Doctor was in there and when he saw that stool go by with that white coconut in it he said, "son, you're not going home – you're going to the Infirmary." When the fellow asked "Why?", the Dr. said, "Because you have worms." "What do you mean I've got worms?" the fellow asked. The Dr. said, "There are a whole lot of white worms in your stool." The guy said, "No, that's coconut." The Dr. said, "No, they're worms, I can tell worms." The guy asked, "Were they wiggling?" The Dr. said, I don't know, I didn't have time to see, but they were worms." Then the Dr. said, "You are going to have to stay in the Infirmary for the weekend until we de-worm you."

Anyway the fellow was mad and he couldn't find his clothes, so my buddy who was there waiting for me found him some clothes because he said he was going home anyway. It was Friday night and the Dr. was gone so he got dressed and came out and got into my car. It was so cold – it was freezing cold and we started down the road in the Chevrolet. We stopped at a service station because I had to put water in the radiator. We had to keep the motor running to keep the car from freezing up. It was so cold that as I was putting water in the radiator some of it froze when it hit the ground. We laughed all the way home about the "worms" in that guy's stool.

While in the CCC's at Index I ran compass and helped the junior foresters cruising timber, etc. The CCC boys normally only worked six hours a day so the junior foresters asked if I would work some overtime and help them with some of their work they would give me compensation. They couldn't pay me, but they said they would give me compensatory time. So I was working eight eight hours a day and sometimes I worked on Saturdays. I worked with them for a couple of months there and they caught up with some of their work. However, the supervisor in the Forest Service wouldn't give me any comp. time because he thought I was trying to pull something on him and so he sent me back up to camp.

I went home that weekend and then I went back up to the foresters. They asked me why I had come back and I told them that the supervisor wouldn't give me time off and he had sent me back up there. Well, it seemed as though they were the bosses and it was just like lighting a stick of dynamite. They jumped on the phone and they worked that supervisor over and had him send up a truck that was going to pick me up and take me to Bellingham to have my teeth pulled.

One hot summer day while I was walking down the road hitchhiking home I stopped by a stream. There was a big pond right where the stream came out with lily pads on it, and on top of one of the lily pads was a lizard. To my surprise, along came a great big dragonfly who made a run for that lizard, curling his tail as if he were going to sting him. The lizard, who had a very long tongue, slapped that tongue out and to my dismay there was a big fight between the dragonfly and the lizard. It was something I had never seen before – nor since – but a little thing I never forgot. I thought that if I had had a camera to take some photos of that little fight and show them on a screen it would be worth a lot of money. It was a thing that would really surprise you and put you way back thousands of years when there were dragons and prehistoric animals that would fight.

My career with the the CCC was just about over . . . I joined in November of 1934 and came out in February of 1936.

Jim Anderson and Dave Strom
End of Illabot Lake - 1936

Chapter V

I got out of the C.C.C. in 1936 because at that time different jobs began to show up and they were picking people out for certain trades. The County Engineer in Bellingham saw my name on a list of unemployed so he took me out of the CCC, which was a wonderful thing. I got $4.00 per day working as an assistant to a bridge engineer. I worked with him about four months and made quite a lot of money, about $400. I had about $500 in my pocket which was considered a lot of money at that time.

I was still going with Marie – we had been going together about a year-and-a-half when I asked her if I should buy a Model A Ford, which was about $300, or get married. We decided to get married although there were still hard times and I didn't know how it would work out.

We were married August 29, 1936 and we lived in the Brunswick Apts. where we paid $15 per month rent. We stayed there about a month and I didn't have any work so we thought we should move out of town. There were some apartments up on James and Caroline streets that a lady was renting, and she said there had to be some work done on them, papering etc. She would let that go towards the rent if we would do the work, so we papered and painted the rooms in trade for rent. We had never done any papering before and it was a job trying to put that paper on the ceiling. We would end up with it on our backs and all over the place, but we finally got it done and then stayed there for a month or two.

I finally had to go on the WPA because I just couldn't find any work. The Scout Executive there noticed that I had done a lot of scouting and he needed two people to work for him. So they sort of donated me to the Boy Scouts of America where I was acting as an assistant to the Scout Executive as camp director. My job was to go out and find boy scout leaders and teach boys in addition to going to school.

Boy Scouts of America - 1938
Bellingham, WA Troop

Canadian Boy Scouts - 1938
Black Mountain Lodge

I liked the Boy Scout work very much and stayed there in the business for four or five years. I ran Silver Lake Scout Camp which is above Maple Falls northeast of Bellingham. I worked there in the sumertime as a Camp Director and I trained boys in wood culture and nature culture, etc. I worked with them a lot and there were a lot of memorable incidents that happened while I was there.

I remember taking a bunch of seventeen-year-old boys up the side of a mountain one time. After we had gone a ways up the mountain and were tired, I sat down on a log to rest. The rest of the boys sat near me and one of the boys came over and said, "Mr. Anderson, there's room for two people on that log so would you move over and let me sit down beside you?" Well, it just so happened that I was sitting on a yellow jacket's hole and when I moved over they just poured out in a thick swarm. We all started running and I told the boys to run downhill, but some of them ran uphill and one of them got stung very badly, all over his entire body including the area around his penis. He was terribly swollen all over. We took him down to camp, but there wasn't a doctor nearby so we took him up to the CCC camp at Glacier to a doctor there where they packed him in ice and pulled the stingers out. They said that cured him and he'd never be bothered by bee stings after that. I remember getting stung once right in the stomach.

While I was in the Boy Scouts they started a new program – Cub Scouts. Cut Scouts had never been heard of before, but they organized groups – or dens – called Lions, Wolves, etc., of boys age 9, 10 and 11. I had to organize these new groups and new ideas and I had four or five fathers to help me out. Together we had a pretty good group going. This was about three or four years after I'd been married and the kids all wanted me to take them on a hike. I said o.k., that we would get some fathers to go along with us and we would go down on Chuckanut Bay out in a cove I knew there. I got my mother to take care of Eleanor and Janet, our daughters, who were quite small and Marie and three of the boys' fathers went with us.

We went down to Chuckanut Bay where there was a spit running out there. The railroad crossed Chuckanut Bay and so there was a bridge there over the tide flats so the railroad track ran right across the Bay. It so happened that where we wanted to go we had to go in the tunnel. I didn't think there would be any trains coming, and I had

24

instructed the boys that if I blew my whistle real loud they were to hit the ditch on the side of the tunnel.

Well, we got half way through the tunnel and sure enough we heard a train whistle and it came right on us. I blew that whistle and all the kids hit the ditch on both sides. Marie was way up at the end and I could just see her in the light. She jumped out from in front of the train just in time. After the train had gone by the boys all got up and they were all muddy and dirty, but we went on through. When we came back we went over the top of the tunnel. I've never forgotten that day – it was one time when the good Lord helped me. I am sure He was right with me, or I would have lost a lot of boys, and possibly my wife. It was the first time I felt the Lord was protecting me.

When I got back to Bellingham and took the kids home there was a big write-up in the *Herald* about my taking those boys through that tunnel and they advised us never to do it again.

While working for the Boy Scouts of America, I was under the supervision of a Mr. Crompton who was the Chief Scout Executive. We all called him "Tyee" which means "chief". He thought a lot of me and we became very good friends.

I wasn't making very much money and was renting a house on James and Caroline streets. Nearby there was a little house sitting back in a lot which I noticed was empty. The City had a claim against it because someone who had owned it before owed some back taxes. I went to the City and asked if it was possible to buy it. They told me to come to the next City Council meeting and make a bid on it. I asked what I should bid on it and was told that there was $400 against it and if I bid $450 on it with $50 down and $10 per month I would probably get it. I went to "Tyee" and told him the situation and he said, "Jimmy, you go right across the street to those Loan Sharks and borrow $50 and I'll co-sign for you. So I did and I went to the City Council and made the bid on the property and they accepted it. So that was the first home I ever owned, or started to own.

The thing that bothered me was the Loan Sharks who were so hot against me and so afraid that I wouldn't pay them back. I had to pay them back $75 for the $50 loan, and they hounded me all the time. I remember fixing up the old house and putting plumbing pipes into it and when I sold it I got about four times what I paid for it.

I also had a job working now and then for a fellow named Ben

Johnson. He was an engineer who hired me to pull chain or hold rod, working evenings. He paid me 50¢ an hour to work with him, which was pretty good for those days. At that same time I also had a job in the sugar beet factory – chase and sample. I had to chase down a ladder and pick up a sample of water from 18 different sections of the mill which I would then take to the chemist. He would test the samples to see if there was any sugar leaking anywhere. Any sugar leaks would show up in those samples and then they would have to shut the mill down and check it out. I always wanted to be able to shut the mill down for some reason, but that only happened once. I really had to move on that job – I had a little box with 18 sets of cans and I picked up a sample from each station and took it up to the chemist to test. That job lasted about six weeks.

Then I had a job in a furniture factory for about six or eight weeks. They were making tables and chairs out of alder. My job was to test the legs – which consisted of cracking them against something. If they broke they were no good. I was supposed to go through about 20 chairs a day. I remember one of the fellows was absent one day and the boss came around and asked me if I would work on both tables. I told him I couldn't put out that many tables, and he said that if I put out half that it would be o.k. So I worked one day and the next day or so the Supervisor came around and looked at the card and saw that I had only done about 20 of them and Oh! he was mad. He was about to fire me over that and I was about ready to walk out when the boss came out and said, "What's going on here?"

I had lost my voice so I couldn't argue very loud, but I told him what had happened. I tell you about a supervisor getting bawled out. I didn't know a boss could bawl out a supervisor so bad. But he told the supervisor to get out of that blankety-blank mill and stay out of there and not come back. I never forgot how he stood up for me on that job.

In 1939 while working in the Boy Scouts we had quite a few older boys in camp, 16 and 17 year old boys, and they wanted to go up to Mount Baker. The Key Executive gave us a station wagon and a car to take about 11 or 12 of them up to a place called Kulshan Cabin that was near Coleman Glacier. The cabin was put there by the Mountaineers for people to enjoy and was quite a big place, so we took the group up to the cabin to stay overnight. It was very near the Coleman

Glacier which is a glacier that is moving all of the time. We stayed there overnight and the next day we walked up to the glacier and could hear it roaring and moving. The weather was very hot and the boys wanted to go out on the glacier, but I said, "No way". I told them that right then at that time with the weather as hot as it was there could be a slide that would take us all out.

The next day as we got ready to go back to camp we met a group of older people coming in, college people, who belonged to the Mountaineers. There were about 27 of them and they were studying to go to college at the normal school in Bellingham.

The group of young men we met crossed that glacier and one of the fellows was yodeling and they were yelling and – believe it or not – that noise started a big slide. The glacier moved down that hill and all 27 people were caught in it. I believe seven of them went into that glacier and died. They were able to get four or five of them out, but there are still some in that glacier who they will never get out, who will come out down below someday. As I took the boys back to camp we talked about how dangerous that glacier was.

That fall I got a job with the Forest Service as lookout on Goat Mountain. While I was a lookout there there were fires all over. There was a young assistant ranger at the Glacier Ranger Station named Don Stickney who was a very nice young fellow. When we were up in the lookout they were searching for those people who were on the glacier and I thanked God for not taking those kids across it because we would have gotten it for sure.

My assignment at Goat Mountain lookout was my first introduction to the Forest Service. I had always wanted to work for them. They hired me because I knew something about angles and compass work. As a fire finder you had to know angles, etc. in order to give directions to a fire. I was there for about two weeks. There were other fellows on other lookouts and we had a telephone line between us so we could talk back and forth, which helped a lot because it was a lonely job up there.

The fellow who was in the lookout before me was named Brown and they took him out on a fire, so I took his place while he was away. One of the fellows on another lookout asked me why didn't I bake a cake? I said I didn't know if I had the stuff there, but looked around and found that I had everything I needed to bake a cake. I decided to make a chocolate cake and spent most of the day mixing up that cake. Somehow I must have gotten too much baking powder or something in the mix. By evening when the cake was baked I made a pudding for it to put on top and I ate some of it that night. It gave me the runs and I was never so sick in my entire life. I must have run up and down those tower steps dozens of times because that cake went right through me.

But I enjoyed that job which was a fine introduction to the Forest Service. I hiked up Goat Mountain and from the lookout I could see Mount Baker Lodge and what was going on up there. I had to make frequent reports to Headquarters.

Chapter VI

The following year I didn't do much. I went back to work for the Boy Scouts that year and then in 1941 I went back to work for the Forest Service. I was supposed to be sent to a lookout way back at a place called Gee Point up the Stillaguamish which was a ten mile hike to get to. When I got to the Ranger Station in June I had a buddy who was on what they called a 21 man fire fighting crew there, a special crew to fight fires. My friend, Dave Stromey said, "Why don't you stay with us – you'll have more fun on the fire fighting crew and we may not have to go to a fire." So instead of going to the lookout I went on the firefighting crew and they found someone else to send up to the lookout.

We weren't in camp very long before we were sent to a forest fire up in the South Fork of the Sauk River at a place called the Lost Mountain area. It was a very rugged area and very tough climbing and we were on that fire for a couple of weeks. We would take a hose and run it way up a tree and put in through a funnel for fighting fire. We would have water running down through a hose for maybe 700 or 800 feet and the pressure would build up so strong that we could put out most any fire. I remember sitting on a rock with another fellow holding a hose when we saw some rabbits running around and we turned the hose on 'em and watched 'em run.

One day lightning hit up above that tree and came down the pipeline and down the hose line and gave us a shock. The lightning was terrible! I remember sitting there one time when lightning stuck right close to me and a friend of mine who was sitting with me . . . his eyes came right out of his head. You just can't imagine how terrible it is to have lightning strike right beside you.

On that fire we had one boss who was a real go-getter. He would take you into any place as he didn't think much of danger. One of the boys he took in there had a tree fall on him which broke his back and we had to pack him out. They thought he would never walk again.

We were on several fires that summer. One was up at Glacier Peak over the mountain in Rapid Creek country. You had to go up over Copper Mountain and drop down on the other side. It was very hard country to get to and it took us most of the day to get to the fire. We all carried what they called K Rations. In these K Rations there was a can of bread, a little bit of fruit, some crackers and a little can of soup – enough to keep a man going for one meal anyway. We ate that and a plane was supposed to drop in some food supplies for us. When we got way back in there we couldn't find the fire and we were stuck without any food. The plane came in the next day to drop some food for us, but couldn't make the drop and so we went back out again because we were hungry.

There was a creek back there that was running full of trout and I remember the cook getting in the creek with those fish to try to catch dinner for us. We had brought frying pans and we built a big fire and started cooking fish in butter for dinner. Finally, when the plane did make a drop of food, the timber was so thick that some of it didn't get to the ground.

I remember the foreman whose name was Rolfe, was a wonderful fellow to work for and he liked his beer. Anyway, a big case of beans or something landed way up on top of a big fir tree which must have been four feet through. I remember Rolfe looking up there and saying, "Jimmy, if that was a case of beer up there I'd take that knife of yours and whittle this tree down until I got it."

I've always remembered these stories and I have always remembered that I was afraid of bees.

We came off that fire a few days later and went back to Glacier. The fire was near the Canadian border and there was a branch of the river from Canada that came in there – the river that runs through Canada. (It's a good thing I'm telling these stories now because it is getting harder to remember the places I've been and the things I have done.) Anyhow it was the Fraser River running down through Canada and it was a branch of that river that ran through where we were. I remember they talked about sturgeons in the river. We could hear them flopping over in the water as they were huge fish, 16 or 17 feet long. We were at that location for three or four days, but we never did find the fire so we came out and went back to the Ranger Station where we stayed for a couple of days.

A few days after that we got a call that there was a big fire up in the Chilliwack, a long way in from the American side. To get into that fire we had to hike over what they call "Hannigan Pass" and down into the Little Chilliwack and beyond. It was a long hike of about 21 miles. Some of us went in over Copper Ridge and hiked down over the hill. It took us a long time to get there because I remember hiking along with a buddy of mine (we knew where we had to go), and we stopped by the lookout.

The other crew was a little ahead of us and after leaving the lookout, Dave and I looked down into the valley and saw a huge bear. It must have been a Grizzly! It had caught a goat and it was kicking and tossing that goat around. I had bragged about shooting a bear, and I had a little 22 revolver with me. Dave kidded me and said, "Do you want to go down and shoot that thing?" I said, "We wouldn't have a chance." The best thing was that we were way up on top of a ridge over a cliff and that bear would have had to come a long way to get to us.

We kept on hiking toward the fire and I remember Dave saying, "Let's have grouse for dinner." There were a lot of ptarmigans (not grouse) around and Dave was trying to shoot one with my revolver. He kept missing and he finally got mad and threw the gun at one and hit it, but he didn't kill it. From then on I never cared much about carrying a small gun with me in the woods because it wasn't big enough to do any good.

We finally caught up with the others and got down into the Little Chilliwack and into camp. (I'll tell more about that later on).

Now, I'm going to back up on this story!

I went to work for the Forest Service that summer. It was about the first of July when we got the fire crew organized. We had been fighting fires all over – as there were so many – 21 up on the Suiattle River alone. They couldn't find enough firefighters and so they did a lot of burning. About every ten days a lightning storm would come through and start new fires, until things just got out of hand.

Once we got to the Chilliwack fire we worked on it for days and days. It wasn't easy making fire lines in that rough and rocky country. We finally got a line around one fire and the boss came over to Dave Stromey and me and said, "You guys sit down here – you've been working too hard. Sit here and guard this piece above you and if you see the fire is going to jump over the line then run up and put it out. Just watch this line and see that no fires jump over it."

I was sitting down with the water and Dave was facing up, watching my back and I was facing the other direction watching his back, from where we could watch the entire line. We didn't get to sit very long when both of us were going after fires that had started all over the place. It was a difficult job and very hard work. The entire crew was getting completely worn out because of being on the job so many hours, including Saturdays and Sundays, with very little sleep at night for almost two months.

Chapter VII

One day up on the Chilliwack we got up early in the morning to fight fire. One of the guides there, I think he was an Indian boy, was going to go up and get some water for the crew. He asked if anyone wanted to go with him, so I decided to take some canteens and get water for the crew.

We started up this rock slide with him just ahead of me. The rocks were very thick and about the size of a table, jagged and every which way. As he passed this one spot he said, "Jimmy, look out for that rock, it's loose." Well, he spoke a split second too late because I had already put my foot on that rock. It rolled over my left leg and smashed it. It bent my leg back and crushed it badly between my ankle and knee. I called him back, wondering why God would let this happen to me. I had never suffered so much in my life.

The guide went back and got the crew and the foreman who came up to help get me out. They were going to have to make a stretcher to haul me out to the trail. I remember the foreman saying they had nothing to give me for the pain, nothing at all, except some "snoose." I didn't want to chew "snoose" but I did. I stuck some under my tongue and it made me very sick.

The crew made a stretcher and got me out to the trail where they had a young, beautiful horse named "Babe". They put me into a stretcher they had on her and tied up my leg. It took them all morning to get me out to the trail and onto that horse, but finally I was on the horse and we started out. The horse had to walk very carefully in order to keep from causing me too much pain.

Along the Chilliwack trail there was what they called the U.S. Cabin where the Forest Service always kept food for horses. We thought we would feed the horse when we got there. That night when we reached the cabin we found that the bears had gotten in and eaten all the food for the horses. I felt so sorry for that horse – so very sorry –

but there was nothing I could do about it.

Dean Brown was with me as I rode that horse. I remember getting up to Hannigan Pass that night and wanted to get off and let the horse rest. And, oh, that was painful. The horse sat down and was so tired it could hardly walk. I'll never forget coming over Hannigan Pass and down the other side. It took two days and one night to get me out of there. At the end of the trail there was a road to Bellingham where there was an ambulance waiting for me.

I remember getting into the ambulance and the young nurse who rode with me. I couldn't figure out why, but she had orders to keep me awake until I got to the hospital. It took a long time to get there, as it was several hours drive up to St. Joseph's Hospital in Bellingham.

We had a doctor by the name of Gil Shannon who was a good doctor. He looked at the leg which was twice it's normal size and didn't know what to do with it. Because the bones were so badly crushed the ride down the trail had shaken it up and caused the bones to cut into the flesh. He didn't know if he could save my leg or not. It took a day and a half to get the swelling down so he could reset the bones. I'll never forget Doc Shannon working on that leg, stretching it out and putting pins it in.

I remember Janet and Eleanor, who were just little girls, coming over and looking at my leg. They didn't know what to make of it. Marie and the girls were staying at my Mother's place at the time. It was late summer, toward the end of August. I was in terrible misery for several days with those pins and I didn't think I could take it. I didn't know why it should have happened.

The nurses at the hospital were mostly Catholic Nuns. One day I called the nurse and in came a beautiful young nun. The sun shone on her face making her look just like an angel. I told her, "I can't take this much more, please give me something for the pain." She asked me some questions and then reached into her pocket and handed me a little tiny pill, not much bigger than a match head. I said, "Sister, that's not going to do me a bit of good, I'm in big pain." She said, "You take that pill Mr. Anderson."

So I took it and waited, and pretty soon I was off in a wonderful world – everything was so wonderful I could hardly believe it. When she came in later I told her how wonderful it was and that it had worked. She told me it was a morphine tablet and she didn't dare give me too much of it, because a person could become addicted. I don't remember how long they gave me that pill.

I remember looking out the window of the hospital one day and seeing a Priest, an older man in his fifties – I was about twenty-five at the time. This Catholic Priest came every day and walked around, and was always reading something. I thought he was just a regular Priest, but the Sister informed me that he was the Superintendent – the big boss – who was running the hospital. He was in charge of all the staff and they had to answer to him.

HAS WHAT IT TAKES—Jimmy Anderson, member of a twenty-man crew fighting fire in the Copper ridge district east of Shuksan, rode a horse out of the fire area last week despite a broken leg.

He broke the limb when he pulled a boulder on top of himself while climbing a rocky slope. Workers carried him on a stretcher for a way and the rest of the long trek out to a waiting ambulance Anderson made on horseback, his leg in a splint.

Anderson is a Bellingham scoutmaster and assistant to Scout Executive Robert E. Crompton.

He was a German. This was right before we went to war, when Hitler was fighting over in Europe. I found out that the Priest had left just before Hitler got into power, but he had five brothers who didn't get out. The Sister told me that he spoke five languages and was very cultured and well educated. She sent him to see me one time and we had a wonderful chat. He told me about all the different languages he spoke and the places he had seen all over the world as a Catholic Priest.

I remember being in the hospital until October. I got to feeling real well, but they wouldn't let me go home. I was given a wheelchair to go around the hospital in, but just didn't know what to do with myself. I tried to get into mischief. I remember one time I started down Pine Street in the wheelchair. I wanted to go to town, but the nurses came and caught me and took me back to the hospital. The head Sister got so angry with me that she said if I didn't behave she was going to send me home. I told her, " 'home' is where I've been wanting to go for a long time."

Well, it wasn't very long before I did get to go home. I had a cast on my leg and two pins in it, and I was walking on crutches. I remember having to take an awful lot of calcium to get back in my bones and build my leg back up. I couldn't do too much, but just walk around, listen to the radio or go up to the Scout Office to see what was going on. I had nothing to do and nothing much happened in that length of time I spent recuperating.

Chapter VIII

It wasn't long until December 7th came and the war broke out. I remember hearing about it while I was sitting on a stool trying to wash myself. I remember hearing the President, Franklin Roosevelt, declare war on Japan, and of course, everything started out then.

I remember going uptown on my crutches one day – it was about a mile up to James Street. It was the second day after Pearl Harbor was attacked. There were Army trucks all over the place and they had one truck full of Filipinos, I think, and I thought that the "Japs" had landed. However, they were just local National Guard.

We had a good big National Guard and so I imagine they took all of them from that point on and put 'em in the Army. They had a lot of soldiers along Chuckanut Bay because there were a lot of Japanese people living there, and they didn't want to take chances with any of them. They were most likely American Japanese working in the canneries, etc., but the Army didn't know that and so picked them all up and sent them to camps of some kind. That probably wasn't the right thing to do, but it was done anyway.

I had to wait until my leg healed, and so I had nothing to do that winter except read and listen to the radio. I think it was in January of 1942 sometime that Dr. Gil Shannon took me up to St. Joseph's Hospital. I suspected that there would be a lot of misery involved. The doctor had an awful time taking those pins out of my leg because they had callused right inside of the bones – but he had to get them out of there. At one time he suggested taking a piece of bone about the size of a match out of my right leg and put it in my left leg. To that I said, "No, Dr., then I would be crippled in both legs and I don't want that." I told him I would take a chance the way it was. He told me that when I got to be about forty years old I'd probably get a little arthritis or rheumatism in that leg. I said I'd take the chance – and you know I never did get arthritis or rheumatism in it.

I put in that winter doing nothing. Finally one day in April I could walk pretty good with a cane and so I went up to the Forest Service and asked them if they had any kind of job I could do. It just happened that the Assistant Supervisor was Newt Field and he said, "Say, Jimmy, we have to open up the Lookouts up around Darrington and those places for AWS stations. We have to have somebody to man them and we wondered if you would go up to a lookout and stay and take care of it?" Well, I just ate that up. I guess I shouldn't have left home so soon, but I wanted to do something. I wasn't going to get much more money working as I was on compensatory time, but I wanted to work.

Chapter IX

I always remember coming through the gate at the Ranger Station in Darrington. I had a coat on my back and a coat slung over my arm and I walked into the office where they made out all kinds of papers. It took them about an hour to take my fingerprints and get all the information they needed from me. Then they put me in a truck and took me right up to the French Creek Lookout.

When I came to Darrington in the spring of 1942 there were three people working in the office for the Forest Service. They were the Ranger, Charles Thurston, Joe Hollingsworth and Nels Bruseth. There was also a fellow named Hough who did the scaling for them up the Suiattle. There wasn't much going on at the time except the logging way up the Sauk.

When I got to the French Creek Lookout there was another fellow working there and the two of us worked shifts. One worked days and one worked nights, as we had to keep watch 24 hours a day, reporting in every hour. If there was a plane coming we had a code that we sent in and had to report the direction it came from and the direction it was going. Of course at night we couldn't always tell the numbers, but we always reported sightings and they would pass the report directly to Seattle.

Most of the planes were our own, but they were worried that maybe a Japanese plane could sneak through the lines somewhere and drop a bomb. At that time they did have some kind of a sheet of thin paper, about the size of an envelope, that they could dump in the woods. When it reached a certain temperature, about 75^0, it would flame up and go into a fire. The U.S. was worried about that, because if the Japanese wanted to start forest fires they could do that.

I guess at one time one of the Japanese planes did get into Oregon somewhere, but it was never publicized for fear it would worry the people. The plane just got in so far and dropped a bomb on a family at a picnic or something, then took off again. I do remember something about that.

That summer I worked in the French Creek Lookout under the direction of Charles Thurston. It was a slow, lonely job and I was sorry after I got there that I hadn't stayed home because I missed Marie and my two little girls. Charles Thurston, the Ranger, was a good Ranger and I didn't mind working for him, although he was a hard man and a hard worker who believed in what he did. I remember one time riding up the road with him, he was smoking a pipe and there was a sign on the side of the road that said "No Smoking In The National Forest," so he stopped the car and knocked out all the ashes from his pipe into the ashtray. He said, "Jimmy, there is one thing I believe in and that is if there is a Law, obey it." He said, "It will keep you straight in the long run." I respected the man for that.

Charles Thurston was the Ranger until the time I moved back up into French Creek and that was about the same time Harold Engles moved back to Darrington. He had been transferred down to Zig Zag National Forest in Oregon in the Hood River country where they had a lot of skiing. He had hurt his back helping people out of ditches in their cars. He was a powerful man and he'd bounce them out of the snow to get them going again. He came back to Darrington when he was a man of about forty and I must have been about twenty-six. He had been hurt and he was a hard man, but I had all the respect in the world for him.

While Harold Engles was the Ranger at Darrington and I had the cast on my leg, there was a fellow staying with me at the Lookout. His name was Jim Plasco, and he was a leftover from the CCC Camp. He was working with me at the time and the Ranger wanted me to go up to Goat Flats to see how much snow there was. I started out about six o'clock one morning with a lunch consisting of a sandwich, an orange and an egg. Seems to me I had a dog with me too! It was about twelve miles to the Ford and from there it would be three and a half miles up on switchbacks to what they call Tupso Pass, which was the start of the climb back into Goat Flats. I walked two or three miles and hit Bandana Lake, which wasn't too far up, and I had just begun to get into the snow. I peeled the orange and ate it as I walked through along, and kept on going until I got up to the Flats. There was plenty of snow up there and I could just see the corner of a cabin I thought, "well this is just about far enough."

As I was turning around to start back the fog started coming in. This scared me because I knew what it was like to be caught in fog in the mountains. You just don't know where you are or what to do. It was a good thing I had peeled the orange, because I found a few orange peelings as I was coming back down and knew that I had been through there. I could see the tops of the telephone line just sticking up out of the snow in places. I figured I was walking on top of about eight or nine feet of snow up there and kept walking until I got down to Tupso Pass. It was two or three miles before I got out of the snow.

At about Four Mile there happened to be a bear eating berries or something right under the trail and I almost stepped on his nose. He must have been just out from hibernation because it was early in the spring. It scared the living daylights out of me and I started running down the trail with the dog and the bear started up the side of the hill. I stopped and looked back up and he stopped and looked at me, and I thought I shouldn't have run from that bear. I thought, "My gosh, how stupid we look – afraid of one another."

I finally made it on down to the lookout. I had started early in the morning and didn't get back until late that night, walking about 20 miles in one day with a cast on my leg. My leg was definitely building up to where it was getting pretty strong and I thought I was going to have to do something about it.

When I returned to the Lookout, Jimmy Plasco called the Ranger Station to tell them I was back. He said, "Well, Jimmy finally got in and he is pooped. He hiked about 12 miles up and 12 miles back, which was quite a hike." The folks at the Ranger Station were worried about me being up there by myself. But that's the way it is in the Forest Service – you spend a lot of time by yourself.

I was completely shot when I got back from Goat Flats that night and the next day I called Harold Engles and told him I would have to go to Bellingham and have the cast taken off my leg, because the muscles were beginning to atrophy. He didn't like it very much because he didn't have any replacements, but they sent an older man by the name of Tollenaar to take my place. I went to Bellingham and had the cast taken off and stayed with my wife and family for a little while. Then I came back to French Creek. That was my first Lookout.

Marie Anderson, Joe Kelly, Harry From,
Janet and Eleanor Anderson - Clear Creek 1942.

While I was on that Lookout with Jim Plasco I got up one morning and took a can to go down to the water hole. We used about 5 gallons of water a day and had to pack it from the water hole which was about 200 or 300 feet below the Lookout. I remember carrying a long barreled 22 revolver with me, although I don't remember why I had it. As I stepped out on the road with the water can this huge animal jumped out in front of me. I thought at first it was a bear, but then I noticed the long tail and realized it was a cougar.

I pulled the revolver out and was going to shoot it, but by the time my hand got down to where I could pull the trigger it was shaking. I don't know whether I hit that cougar or not, because it jumped ten feet and then took off down the road. I went on down and got the water and told Jim Plasco about it when I returned and he got all excited. He was from the hills of Tennessee and he said that if you shoot a wild animal, like a cougar, and wound it, it will wait for you for days and days. He said, "I'm not getting of of this Lookout." It took me a long time to convince him that that was just a fairy tale, and that once you shoot an animal it will never come back.

I stayed at French Creek Lookout throughout the summer and up until close to September. Then I took my annual leave and spent some time with my family before I reported to the Ranger Station. The Ranger just decided then and there to ask Marie if she could stand working with me at the Whitechuck Lookout that winter on the AWS station. They had been up there and put rails all around the walkway and steps so the little girls wouldn't fall out. So we decided to try to stay there that winter.

Jim and Marie Anderson, Bob Machen, Billy Hobson, Eleanor and Janet Anderson – French Creek 1942.

Chapter X

In September we moved to the Whitechuck Lookout to be there during the war. The Sauk River Logging Co. had a logging camp right below us and had about 100 men working there, bucking and falling timber, and they had a railroad up there. Now it is a highway, but at the time it was a railroad. I had my old Model A Ford at the time and I drove my family up. I remember the good times and the rough times we had up there. We were at the Whitechuck Lookout from September of 1942 until April or May of 1943.

When we left for the Whitechuck we knew we were going to be there all winter and so they hauled in a lot of wood for us. In addition to the wood stove we had an oil stove for heating the cabin. I brought along my tobaggon, skis and traps, as I was going to try trapping during the winter.

We also had a radio and a telephone. It was a brand new telephone that wouldn't work and I couldn't figure out why, so I used the radio. I decided to try to repair the telephone and so I took it all apart and put the pieces together again, but it just would not work. I don't know how I discovered it, but the ground for a telephone has to be clear down in the water. I tried driving a stick or rod down into the ground and bringing it back up to the telephone, but it still would not work.

So I decided I could get a good ground by hooking it up to the lightning rod. We just had to remember to unhook it if a lightning storm came along. So I did that and it worked just fine, but I had some kind of a mix-up on it because I could hear the radio sometimes on the telephone.

At this point I'm going to describe what a Lookout is like on the inside and outside . . .

A Lookout is a cabin sitting on top of a tower forty feet high with four big cedar posts holding it up. Inside it is 14 feet by 14 feet and has a catwalk around it which is about 4 feet wide all around the Lookout. Most lookouts have rails or a fence around them about three or four feet high so nobody would fall off. This particular Lookout had extra rails put around by the Forest Service so the kids could be up there and not fall off. It also has steps going up 40 feet to the top, which also had rails so nobody would fall off.

The inside of the Lookout was the living quarters. The firefinder sat on top of a pedestal or little stand about four feet high. It was in the center of the room and fixed so you could move it around. In one corner was a bed. All the beds, stools, stove and things you stood or sat on had big wires running from them out to a copper wire lightning rod. Each lightning rod had to run up each corner of the building to the top where it hooked into a copper steel post and then ran back down the post about 100 feet to a moist place where you could stick the rod into the ground. This was so that when lightning struck it would go right to the ground. When lightning hit near a Lookout it really caused some excitement. When you saw a lightning storm coming you had better be on the bed or the stool or something safe, because if it hit you it would naturally burn you.

The Lookout had small windows all around – about nine inches square – lots of small windows so in case you broke one you could easily replace it. I remember how hard it was to keep all those windows clean and clear so you could see out of them. The firefinder was fixed so you could read Azimuth and vertical on it on a big compass that sat on a map. You moved it around the map, and if you looked through the firefinder at a fire you could give them a vertical reading, a horizontal reading and a space on the map. With these instruments one could pinpoint a fire down to within 40 acres, which was close enough for the smoke chasers.

Underneath the firefinder was a little cupboard in the stand. This held reports for smoke chasing and fires. Each day we had to report the weather, the temperature, direction of the wind and the rainfall – a little weather station. We also had what we called a fuel stick which had to be weighed every day when the humidity and the fuel stick came together. All of our regular chores kept us pretty busy, in addition to spotting airplanes. It was quite exciting in the Lookout at times.

When we first moved up to the Whitechuck Lookout I spent a lot of time preparing for the winter – piling up wood and I had my skis all greased and set up by the cabin along with my traps and everything I

WHITECHUCK LOOKOUT

September 1942 - April 1943

Marie, Janet and Eleanor at the Whitechuck Lookout Cabin, 1942.

Janet Anderson - 1942.

46

Fun In The Snow for
Janet and Eleanor . . .

Jimmy
getting the
winter
wood
supply .

Cabin
at
Whitechuck
Lookout -
1942.

was going to need through the winter – all ready. When we first got to the Lookout the two girls had colds, but it wasn't long before they were clear and strong.

Hunting season had opened and there were hunters all over the place. I remember one of them came in and shot a deer and left it. I went down to check it, but by the time I got there they were gone.

The logging camp down below us was getting ready to shut down for the winter, which they usually did because of snow in the high country. They would normally shut down about the first of October, leaving only one person, either the foreman or superintendent.

I remember the coyotes would chase the deer out onto a point where the Sauk and Whitechuck rivers came together. They would sometimes have six or seven deer down there just across the river and I could hear them. I would take a shot or two with my rifle and the coyotes would disappear.

After hunting season was over it didn't take me very long to get things straightened out. We had a very severe winter that year. I remember that when the snow came and froze – and I wasn't on duty – I would take my skis at midnight, throw my rifle on my back and go way up Dan's Creek. Dan's Creek was a little railroad grade, about a 4% grade, and I would walk about two or three miles up the old road (I had a dog with me) and then put on my skis and ski back down. On a moonlit night it was just beautiful with everything sparkling and just the right grade to slide along smoothly . . . it was a real pleasure trip. I could hear the coyotes howling and it was a wonderful thing to be near to and see nature that way.

Often as I was coming down I would see the coyotes chasing the deer and I would take a shot at 'em with my 306, but not very often because the shells were too expensive. I would ski on down to the Lookout as I always had to report in and tell them where I was going and where I would be all the time. I loved those times!

I would get up on top of the Lookout and the coyotes would play a game with me. They would see how close they could get to the Lookout without being discovered. They would get right up close and sit and watch, and if I opened the door of the Lookout they would run away really fast.

I believe they wanted me to notice them and I remember I was going to try to shoot one of those coyotes but you know they could go so fast that they saw me in that Lookout and they would get away before I got there. So one time I thought I would fool them and I laid the rifle down on the catwalk outside and I opened the door and squatted down inside and when they got in there I figured they wouldn't see me and I could jump outside and grab the rifle. But they were so fast they would see me come out that door and fool me every time. It was a wonderful time!

It was so very snowy and so terribly cold that winter that trees would crack open. I could hear them popping all around and I didn't know what it was at first. I called down below and they told me it was the trees cracking because they were so cold. My two girls and Marie were down below in the nice warm cabin where we had plenty of wood and plenty of food, and didn't have to worry about anything.

We had about four feet of snow that winter and they kept the railroad track open to the logging camp. Sometimes I would go down on the "Lokey" to get groceries and supplies.

I remember the airplanes testing us to see if we were alert. They would come down the Whitechuck Valley just skimming the tops of the trees. I forget what kind of fighters they were, but they could just skim over the top of the Lookout. It would take us some time to report them, and they would be a long ways off by the time we phoned the office and the dispatcher had phoned down to Seattle. We had to measure the time it took for us to call down to the dispatcher and for him to call to Seattle or McChord Air Force Base.

I told the Dispatcher at the office, Edith Bedal, that I was going to try to trap coyotes and asked her how to do it. Edith was an Indian princess who had been raised up the Sauk and had trapped. There was a mountain named after her family who came there in the early days. Edith Bedal had been to school and was the Dispatcher.

Edith told me over the phone how I should trap coyotes. She said to get some old chicken feathers, or dumplings, or something that would make a smell, and spread that on the ground all over. But first I had to set the trap and scatter leaves all over it, and then put the chicken feathers or whatever over top of that. There was a thing on the end of a chain that was called "the dog", which I'd pound into a log that was too heavy for a coyote to drag off.

Anyway, the first time I set a trap way up in the valley the dog was with me and so I told it to go home. I hadn't gotten 200 feet away from that trap when I heard a yelp, and that doggone dog had gotten into that trap. From that time on I left the dog tied up. I went out in another direction the next day and set some traps, putting the "dog" in a chunk of wood so it couldn't be dragged away by coyotes. One coyote just pulled it's foot off and left it, which I thought was too much and no way to do, so I did not try to trap anymore.

I could only be gone for one hour at a time without permission. I'll never forget trying to trap coyotes, which was an experience I had never had before. The valley was thick with them.

I think one of the most beautiful sounds you can hear in the forest is a wolf howl. I remember one silent night up at Black Oak I could hear that howl and it was so beautiful. It let you know that nature was still out there, though it would scare some people, I suppose. There were probably only one or two wolves, but you could tell. A coyote just yaps along and doesn't howl, but the wolf howl will run chills up your spine if you are out there by yourself. Of course, being where I was there was no worry.

If the moon was out in the winter, Marie and I would put on our skis and ski down towards the Whitechuck River, which is only a half mile or less with a few switchbacks. We would ski down, seeing if we could make those switchbacks, and could leave the girls up at the Lookout watching because they could look down and see us skiing. We always made sure one of us was way down the trail and one of us was close to the Lookout in case anything went wrong.

Anyway, one day we were skiing down over the hill and some how we both ended up at the bottom and so we hurried back to the Lookout to check the girls. Janet was missing. We asked Eleanor where she was and she said that Janet had gone to look for "Mama". Hearing that scared me so bad I took off on my skis and got down to the river as fast as I could. The bridge over the river had rails on it and I caught her just as she was tottering on those rails. If she had fallen into the river she would never have been found. I will never forget that! We always watched them from then on to see that they didn't go down that way.

Marie, the girls and I spent about eight months in the Whitechuck Lookout, from September until April. What got us out in April was that I had an attack of appendicitis. I told the bosses that I knew something was wrong and that I had to go down and check it out. They did not like it because they had to find someone else to send up to take my place.

Chapter XI

I went to Mount Vernon to a woman doctor whose name was Hilda Brun. She examined me and said my appendix had to come out. By the time I had the operation they were about to rupture. I had known something was wrong because I had a pain that just came and left, so I knew it wasn't the stomach flu. I ended up staying in Mount Vernon for about two weeks.

When we came back to the Ranger station we stayed there for a little while and then they moved us from the Whitechuck to the French Creek Lookout.

If I remember correctly, the danger of air attacks gradually got over in 1943 while we were working there. Marie was training to be a lookout and I worked on the Guard Station. I was also spending a lot of time up on Three Fingers at the time. I guess there were still some air raid warnings then and we were still being tested out of Seattle. Seven of the planes flew over at one time and buzzed us. They also flew over Higgins, where Mrs. Fleming was the lookout. They tried to give us so much work to do that we couldn't do it all. There were so many planes flying by that all we had time to do was to get and report the directions they were coming from and going to.

We stayed at French Creek that whole summer of 1943. I spent my time working on the trail and cleaning out the road. I also made several trips to Three Fingers that summer. I remember one time Harold Engles sent me and another fellow up to Three Fingers to see if there were any fires up there. The snow had pretty much melted and so we were able to get up to the Lookout. I remember we walked a switchback trail that ran in and out of the canyon to get to Three Fingers and that there were goats on the top milling around.

Elmer, an older man who was with me said, "You had better not go through there because the goats are knocking rocks down." Well, we got halfway across and and sure enough, the goats above us were knocking rocks down. Elmer said, "Don't move or they'll hit you." Well, I couldn't for that and I got out of there. It looked like those goats were throwing rocks at us.

Anyway, we went on up and I got on Three Fingers Lookout for the first time. It had a drop of about 3,000 feet on three sides and it had a ladder on one side to get up to it. This lookout was built by Harry Bedal, Harold Engles, Gerald Ashe and another fellow. Harry took a rock drill in there and drilled holes in the rocks and slowly blew the top off of the mountain until he had a thirty-five or forty foot square flat area, and that is where they built the Lookout.

The mountain was about 6,900 feet in elevation and was considered a pretty high peak. They figured they could watch a lot of area from this lookout. I counted about twenty-seven bear and fifteen or more goats up in that area. It was during the war when there weren't many hunters about and no one to bother them, so they were very thick and they weren't afraid of humans.

On the way out a nanny goat and her kid were on the side of the trail and that little kid got so curious to see what I was like that it came very close to me. Well this upset the nanny who started at me. I picked up a big rock and hit her on the side of the head and it just went "kerplunk". Then she pushed the little kid down over the hill out of sight. So we got by that spot.

When we were part way down from our trip to the Three Fingers Lookout Elmer decided he wanted to make a call to let them know where we were. The telephone line was open that far up and so he was able to hook up to it right there and phone in to the Ranger Station.

While Elmer was sitting there he put his hat down. I noticed a porcupine come running by and I took his hat, threw it and hit the porcupine. The hat was full of quills when I sat it down beside me. When Elmer was through phoning he looked at his hat and saw all those quills and asked where was the porcupine. I told him that it was in his hat. He said, "Boy, that was a close call it came that close to me." He didn't realize I had put the porcupine in his hat.

We had quite an experience coming down from Three Fingers for the first time with the goats and bears and all.

Chapter XII

In April of 1943 when they moved us back to French Creek Lookout it was one of the most enjoyable times of my career in the Forest Service. I had Marie and the family with me and there were no more airplanes to spot. Marie was on the Lookout and I was a guard. It was a perfect life for us! I loved it because I could work on the trail and make trips back in the mountains with the packers – fixing phone lines and Lookouts and maintaining trails, etc.

While working in the French Creek Lookout I was also a guard at headquarters down there. The Ranger told me I was responsible for the entire area down on Boulder and French Creeks and Higgins, etc. I was working almost year round and when I wasn't on duty at the AWS Station I was a guard.

Harold Engles came up to me one time and told me that I was going to have to brush out the old road, cut the brush on both sides from Highway 530 up to the Boulder trail, about four miles. I said, "Man alive, Harold, that will take me a long time to do that off and on." He said, "Well, you've got a long time, just work on it when you haven't any other jobs to do like cleaning up the campground, etc." So I got an axe and started cutting alders on both sides of the road. They were mostly about two or three inches thick and so I just cut 'em and laid 'em down.

I remember there was an old fellow living back in there by the name of Joe Gerkman, an old Spanish-American War veteran who was sort of a hermit. He was in his sixties or seventies at that time. I don't see how he could have made it back there in his cabin with no radio or anything. All he had was a heating stove in a little cabin and not much room. I could never understand how an old man could live like that. I understand that he was pretty well off, too, getting a pension. He had a big garden there and he made raspberry wine. He wanted me to kill the deer who came and ate his grass, etc., which I couldn't do, so he built a huge high fence all the way around his garden to keep them out of his raspberries.

I remember him coming out one time to talk to me. He was a German and he spoke very broken English. He said to me, "Now Jimmy, when you come to work I'm going to have a wheelbarrow full of wood for you about 100 feet from the cabin and you can wheel it up for me." So I would do that for him and he would say, "You have to have a drink of wine." He had a little glass of wine ready for me and though I didn't care too much about wine, I had a little drink of it.

Anyway, I walked back up the road and worked until noon and then went on back up to the Lookout for dinner and he'd have that little glass of wine for me when I wheeled in the wood from the other direction.

This one morning it seemed that I made about six trips back and forth. I had a little dog at the Lookout that belonged to Eleanor and Janet. It was a very smart and friendly little dog who followed me to work and stayed with me. One day when I went to work and the dog was with me – a Friday, I think – and was coming home that evening I had to stop and take the glass of wine. It began to have an effect on me and the next thing I knew I looked up the road and saw a dozen culverts going around and around and I could tell right then that I had had too much wine.

I remember the little dog running between my legs chasing a jack rabbit. When I got to the Lookout, Marie said, "there's something wrong with you," to which I replied "I know, I just don't feel well." Then she asked, "where is the dog?" I told her that I didn't know the dog had been with me. When I went into the cabin to lie down the girls got after me for not bringing their dog home. That night when the dog was still missing the girls were beginning to get pretty upset and were about to cry for fear I had lost their dog.

The next morning Newt Field and Harold Engles came up to give me a training session on the firefinder, showing me how to use it and teaching me some of the things I needed to know how to do. When Newt came up he had that dog in his car and when I asked him where he found it he told me, "That dog was sitting down there on your tools right where you left them – she was waiting for you to come to work. She had been lost and didn't know where you were and she was just going to stay there until you came back because she knew you'd be back to work." I opened the door and the dog came in and from that time on she never left the kids. I'll never forget that dog and I'll never forget old Joe and his wine.

I was a fire guard and worked in other places while Marie worked in the Lookout. I did other Forest Service jobs like working on the trails or helping pack materials back into Three Fingers, etc. I remember that I was sent back into Three Fingers about three times that summer. There was a pack string with Harry From, Dutch Tollenaar or whoever was going back in there and I remember they sent Mrs. Tucker back into Goat Flats where she was supposed to be taking care of a Lookout up there.

They sent me up with Harry From to set up a Lookout on a ridge just south of Goat Flats. The Three Fingers Lookout was probably about two miles up above Goat Flats and they didn't want Mrs. Tucker going up to that Lookout because it was too dangerous for her. We started up one time with the packer and seven mules and all the equipment that was needed for the Lookout for the Goat Flats Guard Station. On the way I opened an air mail letter that I had gotten from my buddy and that red and white air mail letter spooked one of the mules. "Jack" panicked and started bucking and kicking around and we had a terrible time calming him down!

By the time we finally got him quieted down we had supplies scattered all over everywhere. We had had the stove in one piece at the time and stuck on one pack, but it didn't work and so we took it apart and packed it on somehow to take it back up to the Lookout. We headed for the Lookout with the pack string and we got up there o.k., but forgot the four bolts that held the stove together. Preston Howell, who was one of the packers, had a fit because we didn't have the bolts to put that stove together.

There were two little lakes up there called Columbine Lake and Noble Lake. One day Harry From and I decided to go swimming in one of them. The lakes were small – not much more than half an acre each and only about six or seven feet deep. The snow was all gone and there were trout in them. Somehow the trout had gotten in these lakes. While we were swimming a big horsefly bit Harry and he took that horsefly and threw it out in the lake where a great big trout jumped up and took it. That excited us, so we got dressed and Harry, who was quite a fisherman, grabbed his pole and started catching fish for supper.

While we were doing that David Tucker, who was about ten years old, was down in the creek and he was kicking his feet around. He lifted up one foot and he had a big trout between his toes and he said, "Look what I've caught." That just gives you an idea about how thick those trout were in the little lake.

We stayed there overnight and the next day I went on up on the ridge and set up a little platform to set the firefinder on. It was a small firefinder, what they called an emergency one, and Harry came along with the telephone. When we got up there we had to find a ground for the telephone. I'd discovered a long time ago that if you chip around a tree and the sap from the tree goes down into the ground far enough to make it into water, it will work as a ground. Those metallic telephone lines had to have a ground – a single line with one ground and you cranked it to get electricity into the line and then you could talk.

I sat there giving them the instructions and I would talk to Higgins and then I would talk to Pilchuck so that Mrs. Tucker could swing the firefinder and pretty well locate it. I do remember that as being one of my best times in the Forest Service.

In 1943 while at the French Creek Lookout Harold Engles called me and told me I was to go with Dutch Tollenaar, the packer, and Byard Tucker and another young fellow to take a pack string of food back into Goat Flats for Mrs. Tucker. We left the trailhead early in the morning and I told Marie I would call her at the Ford. The Ford was about twelve miles up the trail and there was a cabin with a telephone where I could call Marie and the girls at the Lookout.

I remember the names of some of the mules from the pack train, but not all of them because it was so long ago. The lead horse was named "Charlie." Then there was "Bonney" and "Mabel" and "Jack", plus three other mules making seven in all. They were all loaded with food and supplies that Mrs. Tucker had called for. We traveled until we hit the Ford at about ten o'clock in the morning. It was a good place to let the horses rest a little. I decided I would go in and call Marie and tell her how far I was up the trail.

Well, "Mabel" had gone after the food and when she rested she flopped down and put her rump up against the cabin. I mentioned before that the phones had a ground that ran down into the ground and the phone was inside the cabin. When I cranked up the phone it ran an electrical shock through there and it hit "Mabel" who was loaded with butter and eggs, etc. It shocked her and she got scared and started bucking and kicking, scaring all the rest of the mules. Then she started down the creek throwing eggs, butter and the pack equipment all over the place.

Dutch and Byard went down the creek to head off those mules and then we had to go clear down the trail to get the rest of them to keep them from going back to camp. Finally we got them all back together and Dutch, who had an odd way of speaking said, "Now, Jimmy you can go back down the creek and pick up all the butter and eggs or what's left of it." There were about fourteen pounds of butter, etc.

Dutch usually swore a lot, but we had a preacher's son with us and when I said to him, "Dutch, I didn't hear you swear any" he said, "I wouldn't dare." Byard got quite a kick out of that. Besides the exciting moment when the mules panicked we made the trip all right. That has happened two or three times in my life with mules.

Dutch was a good packer, and to be a good packer you have to know exactly how to pack those mules with a diamond hitch and balanced weight on both sides. One thing about mules is that while you can ride them you have to let them make their own way. A mule can see much better than a human and at night you can ride those mules who are so sure footed that when they put their feet down they are sure it will be safe. They will not cross a bridge or anything unless they smell around it and sniff it out.

Anyhow, we got the mules and everything up to Goat Flats meadow – a beautiful place with goats and bear and everything – about two o'clock. When we got there the horseflies were terribly thick and they bothered the mules so much that we didn't know what to do. We fed them and I called the Ranger Station. Someone there suggested we get a rag drenched in kerosene and wring it out and very lightly wipe it on the hair of the mules.

By the time we started back to Darrington it was late afternoon. I remember I was riding "Bonney" down the Boulder Creek Trail when a young bear cub ran underneath her neck and into the brush. I was afraid that it would panic her, but because it happened so quickly I don't believe she even noticed it. A bear will usually panic a mule.

On the way back down I came to one spot on the trail that dropped straight down below and the other part of the trail went straight up. You couldn't get off the mule – when you got there you just had to stay on the mule. I hollered to Dutch and said that maybe I should get off of the mule but he said I was safer on the mule than I would be on the trail. He said, "You just leave the mule alone and she will take you safely out of there." He continued, "If you notice how careful she is, she is not going to trip, she is not going to fall, she watches every step and she can do this at night or any time and can see much better than the average person." It was quite a ride, but we made it safely out of there. It must have been about 8 or 9 o'clock that evening when we got back down to the Trailhead Camp.

During the War most of the Forest Service trails and the National Parks were closed to travel because they didn't have enough men to patrol them, and of course they were worried about sabotage. That was while I was in the French Creek Lookout. The Ranger called up one day and said, "Jimmy, there's somebody up in there who is not supposed to be there, we don't know who, so we want you to go up and find him. Wait for Ollie, the Game Warden."

Ollie came on up to the Lookout and we headed out to go find out who it was. We drove up to the end of the road and started hiking from there. In the first cabin we came to we could hear voices. We went up to the cabin and hollered at them. There was a man and a woman in there and the woman was scolding the man because she thought he had pushed her into the river. They had all their clothes off and were drying them there by the fire. The Warden went up and told them that they had to come out of there immediately, that they weren't supposed to be there and that he would wait for them.

So we waited about an hour until their clothes dried and they got dressed, and we took them out. The man, I can't remember his name, was a policeman in Seattle. He said that he had a right to go any place because he was a policeman. We soon straightened him out and told him that no one could go into the National Forest during the war without a permit from the Ranger or some authority. That was the first experience I had having to run someone down in the forest, but every now and then I had to go investigate and find out why certain people were in there.

In 1945 Harold Engles decided that Eleanor had to go to school and we would have to come down. He fixed up a cabin at the Ranger

Station for us to use for the winter and we stayed there so that Eleanor could go to school, and I was put into other kinds of work.

Residence at Darrington Ranger Station
1943-1946

Chapter XIII

That winter the Forest Service formed a cruising team for the Mount Baker National Forest and there were three of us who did all the cruising for the entire district – Bob Mealy, Joe Kelly and myself. We cruised all over and I loved it because it taught me how to measure trees, to size them up by using a Biltmore Stick holding it up to a tree to get the height of it and then I'd get the diameter of it. I learned to do this and could measure within about 10% of the tree's actual size.

We also had to grade the trees, i.e. whether it was a cull (a tree we couldn't use for anything but wood), or a No. 1 log which was a very good log with knots in it. We graded them 1, 2 and 3. A number 3 could make lumber, but very poor lumber. Then they had what they called a peeler, which was the best kind of a tree or log you could get. They could peel it and use it for plywood.

The first trees that we cruised were big old four, five and six foot in diameter trees in the Suiattle. We spent the winter cruising up through there and I enjoyed it very much. When we were cruising timber during the war the Navy wanted most of the trees for something they were doing. Bob Mealy, Joe Kelly and I spent all that winter of 1943 and 1944 cruising timber in that area. We had a formula that we'd use to multiply it and make it up into acres.

When I wasn't out cruising timber I was in the station acting as what they called a Headquarter's Guard. Now the Headquarter's Guard duty was to inspect the fire cache at all the logging works. Every outfit that logged had to have a box with all the fire tools in it called a fire cache. In that box they had to have a couple of crosscut saws, a couple of axes, a couple hoses and what we called a "Pulaski". A "Pulaski" was a tool that had an axe on one side and grub hoe on the other. They also had to have a five gallon pack can for packing water into a fire. I would go to these logging outfits (there were about nine in the Darrington area) and inspect the cache of tools. Then I'd seal them up so they wouldn't be gotten into so they would be that way each time I came around for inspection.

Another job I had was to help the packer and I also kept the fire cache warehouse where we had all sorts of fire tools, fire pumps and oil pipes. I was to keep them clean and ready to go at a moment's notice. I enjoyed that job quite a bit and was on it during the summer of 1944.

To go back to when I was cruising . . . Once I was cruising the side of Higgins by myself, looking over some timber to be sold and making a line around a patch of timber. When lunch time came I found a beautiful little mossy spot by a stream and sat down there to eat, and it was so pleasant. I sat there watching as the water rolled over little rocks and pebbles making a gurgling sound.

As I sat there I noticed a large water bug coming downstream, a beetle, about an inch and a half long. I noticed that as it came down it would turn over every little rock that it came to and try to hide under it or something. I couldn't figure out why he was acting like this and so I watched him as he made his way along the stream bed for about four or five feet. He was definitely running and hiding, but I couldn't figure out what was happening.

Before long I noticed a little shrew making its way down the stream. A shrew is a little animal shaped like a mole but smaller and they are mean little animals who have to eat ten times their weight each day. I had a fellow tell me that one attacked him on a road one time. They are so aggressive and they are unusual in that they will eat worms or just about anything. He was after that beetle and so he also turned the rocks over as he came down the stream.

I was thinking, there is a whole little world out there that we humans know so little about and seldom notice. There are lots of little things that happen out there that if we knew about, and could tell stories about, would be very interesting. The moles, mice, butterflies and all the little animals and insects that make up the underworld of the forest make a very fascinating story.

Chapter XIV

In the summer of 1944 when I was just beginning to learn how to use a grader, I was sent to a big fire in California in a place called Laguna National Forest, way down near the Mexican border, above the Sierra Desert. The forest there consisted mainly of Greasewood and Manzanita. That was quite an experience for me!

Several of us were shipped down there – Bob Mealy and myself from the Mount Baker and Hornbeck from Glacier. We were to act as Sector bosses on the fire. The fire consisted of 55,000 acres, over 55 square miles. It was so large that each section had to have a sector boss. I was sector boss on the Southwest section of the fire and a local man was to be my guide.

To go back a bit, they put us on a C-47 or what the Army called a flying boxcar in which half the seats were broken. It kind of scared us because we got about half way down there and one motor started cutting out, but we finally made it and they shipped us right up to the fire.

Our fire crews consisted of either soldiers, sailors or marines who had been taken right off of shore leave. Most of the soldiers had been trained to go to war and were through with their training, and were getting ready to be shipped overseas. They were a pretty rough bunch of people.

I had about 75 men in my crew which I organized into groups for what was called "the hunt and peck system" for making a fire trail. The first group would have axes and the second group might have a Pulaski. The next group would have hoes or a grub hoe and the next group would have shovels. The first man in the group would go along and just lop off a branch or two and the greasewood and manzanita was so thick that you could almost walk on top of it.

At that time I took the crew up around the fire and the guide was supposed to take me close to where the fire was burning. We started out and walked most of the day, but never got to the head of the fire.

By the time we did get there the fire had already gone six miles further than it was supposed to. We came to a spot where you could look out over the Mojave Desert. I could see a black spot out there and I asked the guide what it was. It made me feel so sick and hurt when he answered, "That is the only tree in the National Forest." My heart fell right into my stomach and I felt so blue because I was working in a place where there was no forest at all.

I figured they needed that for a fire shed or rather a water shed in the winter time for Los Angeles and different places. That fire was so big and the crews so large that we had many motor vehicles and airplanes on it. We had six airplanes flying over to keep us updated on the fire and I remember someone telling me that they spent $6,000 for sparkplugs alone for the Cats, trucks and other vehicles. There must have been four or five thousand servicemen there – Army, Navy and Marines all "hepped up" and ready to go to war, and it took quite a bit to quiet them down.

I remember this one crew I was supposed to take out. We had to go up over the mountains and down the other side to get to where we were going. There were some sailors the Navy had sent in to help us. These boys had been on a weekend leave and had lived it up and had a pretty rough time. When they got into camp they were pushed out on this fire with hangovers and everything else.

Later on one of the sailors said to me, "You know I looked at you Rangers and figured you were a pretty soft bunch of people and that we would wear you out in about half a day and we'd be able to take it easy. But, we sure got fooled because we found out that you are a tough bunch." To that I said, "Well look – you got fooled because this is my job. You aren't going to wear me out because this is the kind of work I do and I hike all the time . . . I can go all day and all night and all the next day hiking. I'm in pretty good shape for my age."

One of the sailors kept on talking as we walked. We had to go down around the fire and down around another way. It was a rocky trail and it was hard going. We walked and walked carrying those tools all the way. It was getting near the middle of the day when one of the sailors fell and broke his ankle. We weren't sure just what to do and so we stopped the whole crew and radioed to the base camp to send out a stretcher and some guys to pack him out.

We waited a while and pretty soon a single Marine came along.

This fellow was in excellent physical condition . . . I had never seen a man who was better built. He must have weighed about 250 pounds and was over 6 feet tall, all tanned and in perfect condition. You could see the power and pride in this man as he said, "Where is this Sailor who has a broken ankle?" I said, "where is the crew to pack him out?" He said, "I'm it," and with that he put that Sailor up over his shoulder and started down through the rocks with him.

Let me tell you, the rest of the Sailors didn't like that at all, as the Sailors and Marines don't like each other one bit. There were remarks from some of the guys like, "Aw, he's just showing off," and all that stuff. Anyway, he took him on down to the camp for us.

By the time we reached the base camp awhile later one of the sailors with us just dropped in the shade because he just couldn't go any farther. When he fell, half of him was in the shade and the other half was in the sun. He asked a buddy to help him get into the shade and his buddy barely had the strength to help him because he was so tired out. It kind of tickled me in a way, but I felt sorry for one of these Sailors who thought he was so tough and had been sent out there in his tennis shoes . . . he was completely worn out. He worked in the Commissary in the Navy and was pretty soft.

The next day I took a bunch of Marines out with me, and let me tell you they were a tough bunch of fellows. There were seventy-five of them and we started them out the same way – with axes, Pulaskis, shovels, etc. – like I did the other crew. I had to do some real work with that crew. What surprised me was that a couple of Marines came in with one of those great big Cats to try to build fire trails. I tell you I had never seen such a tough bunch of men in my life – the way they handled those great big dozers and stuff, pushing those rocks around really amazed me.

The Marines did a lot of fighting amongst themselves, and I couldn't figure it out. They would be swearing at one another, cussing at one another and using every kind of name you could think of, using some very strong language. I asked the Lieutenant what was the matter with those men and he told me they had been conditioned to go fight a war and that was where they would be going in about two weeks. They would board a ship and be sent to one of the islands where the Japs had landed and were going in to take that island. I've never forgotten that tough bunch of Marines. We got down out of there and the two Cats were parked two fellows jumped out of one Cat and started fighting, and the Lieutenant had to talk them out of it. Every day I had a different crew, which was interesting in a way, but I only got about six hours sleep at night and every morning I would have to get up early and pack my lunch and take another crew out. It got to be pretty hard after a couple of weeks.

I remember taking one crew down to a place which had been cleared out and where there was a big pile of rags and junk everywhere. I asked the guide what-in-the-world had gone on here. The guide told me the story . . . In Los Angeles they had a whorehouse or something that the Sailors and all would go to and there were a lot of married men who would go there. Some of the wives and women of L.A. got together and drove those women out of town. They came up here – miles and miles from L.A. – and put up a hotel or motel and worked from here.

The guide told me that didn't stop them and so the wives and women got together and went up there and burned the motel down. This was what was left of it. They always spoke of the "rag dump" and that was the "rag dump" and it was used as a landmark for a long time.

I stayed on that fire for a couple of weeks and I was pretty well worn out, so they put us on a bus and we started toward home. They told us we were going somewhere for a little R&R for a few days. I didn't care about that because I just wanted to get home. We got as far as Shasta, which was a beautiful place, and they kept us there for a couple of days to rest up. While there we could do anything we wanted to do, including getting a pickup to drive into town. At that time in California you were allowed to smoke while traveling. I nearly burnt up the pickup because I did smoke, and I dropped a cigarette behind the seat which my buddy and I had an awful time finding and putting out.

On the way home we stopped in Hollywood and went into this big beautiful restaurant that had natural forests and waterfalls coming right out of the walls. I've never forgotten it because they had birds in there as well and it was so beautiful . . . just like walking into another world. We were told that the man who built the restaurant was very poor at one time and had a standing rule that anyone who was hungry could come in and be fed.

We started out for home and the bus would break down and it took us a long time. I finally made it to Seattle where I got on another bus headed for home, and it felt so good to be going home. There were two ladies sitting in front of me in the bus and we could see the mountains from the highway. I could see Three Fingers. One of the ladies remarked, "Oh, how wicked those mountains look." They were talking about how wicked and terrible it must be up there. I just leaned over and said, "That is my home and it is the most beautiful place in the world, and when I get there I don't believe I'll ever leave again."

There is a little story I forgot to tell about the Marines . . . I do remember how hard and rough they looked, but they all had music in them somewhere. I remember how they sang, as if they knew that when they got overseas they were going to die. They knew they were going to war and they just didn't know how to take it. They would sing and then a group way across the valley would sing "one more beer for the four of us," and another group on the other side would answer singing, "Glory be to God there are no more of us," and then on the other side of the canyon would come up a single voice singing, "I was drunk last night and drunk the night before," to which another group would sing, "Glory be there are no more of us, more of us, more of us." My heart went out to those Marines because I knew they felt as if they were going on their last trip. I felt so sorry for them it made me hurt in a way I can't describe.

After the fire season was over that fall I had a job laying out a timber sale on what they called Peek-a-Boo Ridge. This part of the story may be a little dry because it's not really a big thing. A timber sale consists of a patch of maybe thirty or forty acres somewhere up on the mountain and there may be twenty to thirty million board feet on it. The timber sale officer, myself, would walk up to the location and look for a place to set a spar tree.

A spar tree is a tree about ninety feet tall where a high climber goes and cuts all the branches off and puts a bull block up on the top. A bull block is a very large pulley that the loggers run their cables through. There are four guy lines that are put through the top and then anchored to stumps on the ground so the spar tree won't move when they are pulling the logs in. This is an important part of the job because you really have to know how to pick a spot for a spar tree. It has to be set right in the middle of the timber patch where you can reach all of the timber in the area, maybe a thousand feet from that spot and pull in the logs.

The next step is to take a surveyor's compass and walk around the edge of it, shooting angles with a compass and marking them down in a book, taking that back to the office where you draw it out on paper. Next you have to tag out a route where a road can be built to reach the timber. The road usually had switchbacks and its a little hard to explain the figuring of this. You take your Adney and set it about 7% adverse and go out with it and then you come out on a logging road somewhere for the logging trucks to drive up.

This can be a long process, and this particular timber sale on the side of Peek-a-Boo Ridge took me about three or four months to lay out. Peek-a-Boo Ridge is the mountain about ten or twelve miles southeast of the town of Darrington. At that time timber was selling for around $15 per thousand board feet. The fellow who bid on it thought that he had bid too much and asked that it be put up on an oral bid at the Ranger Station where other people could bid on it. They did that and it went up to about sixty thousand. From then on timber prices started going up. I spent the winter on timber sales, laying out and tagging roads in different areas for them to build – all at a 7% adverse grade.

There was another big fire I went on late in 1944 in Shasta National Forest which must have burned 100 acres or so – all pine. I was sent down there as a Sector boss, but the fire was just about out by the time I got there. The timber from that fire had been sold since the fire had burned through there so fast that it had just scorced the pine, burning the underbrush as it went through.

A sale contract was made with Diamond Match Co. They had a new system for falling trees that I had never seen before. They ran chainsaws off of track caterpillars that ran compressed air and the saws ran like jackhammers only they were chain saws. You could look over in there and see those trees going down one after another. They had several Cats lined up systematically and they knew which way the trees would go. There were three people to each Cat. Two of them packed air hoses out to the trees and one would be there to size the tree up and see which way it was going to fall. The others would come in and put the undercut in the tree and fall it. When you got back out aways and watched it, it looked like a big hayfork cutting those trees.

The crew I had were Army specialists, older people in their thirties, who were educated and whose jobs in the Army had been to carry radar detecting machines on their backs. I asked one of them one time about the machines and he said they cost about a million dollars apiece. I asked why nobody ever tried to go "over the hill" with one. He said nobody had ever tried to steal one because the government was the only one who used them. These fellows were very educated, but they weren't very good firefighters because they had been in the office too much. I gave them tools and walked them around the fire a few times, and thought it was a good thing I didn't have to fight them too much.

I was only on that fire for about a week when the rain came and we got it out pretty quick.

Chapter XV

This is a story that happened back in about 1944. That year we had a road crew that stayed up at Bedal Campground throughout the summer. There was a supression crew that stayed up there as well and so we brought in two old CCC bunkhouses – which were the kind you put together in pieces. They were good and sturdy, having to be able to withstand the winter.

Somehow when the road crew and the supression crew left there that fall they forgot to brace up the cabins so that the snow wouldn't smash 'em down. Harold Engles thought we should go up there and brace them up. There was already about two feet of snow on the ground and the only way to get there was by skis. So Joe Hollingsworth, Nels Bruseth, Harold Engles and I put on our skis and headed up there to shovel the show off the roof and put some braces on the cabins.

I had a shovel tied to my pack crosswise and it made a very awkward pack along with my sleeping bag and other things. The shovel handle kind of ran down my back there. Anyway, we were skiing along pretty good, and you know you can't hear too much in the snow as it cushions sound a little. It was about seventeen miles up there. We got up to where the Mt. Pugh trail takes off, about ten miles up the road, and the road goes up over a hill and then back down and there was a long coasting hill down the other side.

The rest of the group got a little ahead of me. I stumbled and fell and my skis crossed and that shovel stuck into the snow in a position that was very hard and embarrassing. I hollered at Harold and the others but they couldn't hear a thing and just kept right on skiing, and didn't look back.

Believe it or not I had to take my skis off because I was in such a bind. I was finally able to get out of my skis and I took my pack off, feeling pretty well irritated at them – to a point where it made me a little upset – because they wouldn't stop for me. I had to unpack

Jim Anderson and Nels Bruseth
at Boulder Camp Shelter - 1946.

everything and repack it again, and by the time I got my skis on and got going it took me several miles to catch up with them. When I did they said, "Where have you been?" I came close to blowing my top because they hadn't stopped to help me or anything. But that was all right.

We went on up to the Bedal Campground and got the snow off the roof and spent the night there since we weren't able to do all the work in one evening. The next day we finished clearing snow from the roof and braced the building up real well so the snow wouldn't break it down, then got our skis on and headed out. They had four to five feet of snowfall up there that winter. That was another experience I'll never forget.

As I mentioned earlier, during the winter of 1944 and 1945 I did a lot of different jobs. One morning Nels Bruseth came in early and said, "Yimmy, you and I are going to go up Squire Creek working on that trail to open it up." I couldn't figure out why we would want to do that because it was so late in the year. He said I was to take a crosscut saw and my snowshoes, and he would carry an axe and the skis. I just didn't know what he had in mind, but we started up the trail. A couple of miles up there was a large Alder across the trail. I was ready to take

Nels Bruseth and Jack Swilling
Four Mile shelter on Squire Creek - July 1946.

my cross-cut saw out to saw a piece of it down so the mules could get through, but Nels said, "No, you keep the saw, I'll fix it."

He took his axe and chopped a great big notch down in it pretty low and stepped over it, saying that the mules could step over it now. We went on and pulled branches out of the trail until we got to what we called the Slab Rock shelter. It was up close to Squire Creek Pass and was used years ago as a base camp for working on the trail. Nels had it in mind that we were going to Cedar Basin, which had a lot of snow in it, and that we were going to ski around up there. I put on my snowshoes and tracked around there a little bit but I didn't do any skiing. Nels wanted to go up and look around and that was the main thing that he had in mind in working on that trail.

We turned around and headed back out, getting home that evening. Harold Engles asked how far we had gotten and Nels told him we had been all the way to Cedar Basin. Harold said, "You fellows couldn't have found much in the trail," and Nels said, "Yes, we found one log that we took care of." That was all that was said about that. When Nels went out he didn't have just work on his mind – he also had some nature to think about.

I have to be very careful with this next story I am going to tell because I am bringing some people into it who might take the story wrong. I don't know. A few years ago a friend of mine named Andy Holland wrote a book called "Switchback". In the book he talked about a fire in the Chilliwack which was quite a story, but he didn't tell it all. I asked him why he didn't and he said he was afraid of being criticized over what he said. But, I'm going to tell it like it was, and I told my grandson just exactly what I was going to do. It is going to be quite a long story, but it is very interesting. But I won't start with that right now.

One day in July of 1945 the Ranger called me and told me I was to go to a fire back in the Chilliwack. I hadn't been back in the Chilliwack for six or eight years, since I had crushed my leg there. But I had been hiking all the time and I was in excellent shape. He told me to get my pack and go to Bellingham where I was going to take a small float plane back into Lake Chilliwack. There were also two creeks there – the Big Chilliwack and the Little Chilliwack, and this fire was on the Little Chilliwack which wasn't very far from the Canadian border.

I went to Bellingham and got on the plane. We got into the lake about noon and I saw there was a cabin up there on the side of the hill and I wondered what that cabin was. There were some old abandoned buildings in there as well. I found out that a few years back, during the war, there was a group called the "Dukaboor" who were Russian people who protested the war. The way those people protested anything was to take off all their clothes and go naked. The Mounted Police had a terrible time with them.

They were just a different bunch of people who didn't want to go with the laws, so they decided they would go way back up in the Chilliwack and build themselves a lodge. In that lodge, which was one big building, they had a lot of little rooms facing a large area where families could gather and socialize. It seems there was someone who was an electrical engineer because there were a lot of generators and electric motors that someone had been working on. I also found an old ICS library on electrical engineering that had been left behind. I was told that the Mounted Police had come in and took them out. I don't know why they did, but that was the story and they had a Mounted Police posted at the cabin to keep watch over the area.

I walked on up the trail two or three miles to get into the Little

Chilliwack fire. I was supposed to be a chief scout on that fire. I don't know how big it was – probably 40 acres or perhaps more that had burnt. They had a lot of men on that fire, rough and tough loggers who were in pretty good shape. The fire boss told me to try and walk around the lake and map it as I went. I took a compass and I did the best I could. It took me about a day to walk around the fire and map it because it was a very rough area, rough terrain and rocks, etc. Anyway, coming around there I noticed a dead deer, which I didn't pay any attention to at the time.

Before I continue this story I should tell you that the Army had dropped a bunch of black paratroopers in there. They were people from the south and were very well trained paratroopers who had jumped for the Army.

They shouldn't have dropped them where they did because the area was infested with big snags and big trees. But, they dropped about fifty men, brave and tough men, but some of them got hung up in the trees. They each had two sets of parachutes – a silk parachute and a jumping chute. I don't know what they did with the other parachute, I suppose it was for a different kind of a job. When the paratroopers jumped one of them had his back broken and another got caught up in a tree. It took about eight or ten of the other fellows to pack them out to the lake where the plane was supposed to pick them up.

The paratroopers all came together in camp and they were supposed to fight the fire, but were afraid to go out into the woods. This was all new country to them, being from the south, they knew nothing about this area at all.

Anyway, one night, two or three days after I had gotten in, the Supervisor, Harold Engles and the Ranger came in to discuss procedures for the next day for fighting the fire – what to do. The camp cook had just put on a big kettle of water in order to make syrup for the next day for hot cakes. We were all sitting around the fire when the Ranger asked me if I had seen that dead deer out there. I said that I had, and he asked me if I had any ideas about why it had died or if I'd noticed any injuries on it. I said that I thought it had probably been killed by a cougar or something.

When the people around the fire heard me talking about the dead deer that might have been killed by a cougar, they all got closer to the fire. One young fellow got too close and his sleeping bag caught on fire. One of the other guys hollered at him, "You're on fire!" The cook had taken the kettle of hot water off and had put sugar in it to make the syrup, but when he heard "fire" and realized what was going on he threw the container of water on that guy to put the fire out.

Two other fellows got up and got hold of that guy and swung him back and forth and clear out into the creek. The poor guy had been badly abused and he came out of there all tired and wet and sore and he had just had it. He said, "First thing they do is put me in the Army and teach me to jump, which was bad enough, then they bring me way out here to jump into a bunch of snags and brush where there's lions and bears and snakes." He said, "I just don't know – and then they've got me down here sleeping in a bag and they try to burn me and drown me. If I ever get back to North Carolina I'll never leave, never leave."

Of course that hit us all! The next day the Supervisor came to Andy Holland and said, "Andy, you take the rest of these fellows out of here, being they are scared we just don't need them." So the next day Holland lined them up and gave them each a sleeping bag which they were supposed to carry out with them to the end of the trail about 20 miles away. They just carried those sleeping bags about half way down that trail and dumped them. As they went out they chanted the whole route, "supper, supper, supper." Andy always considered himself a good hiker, but he was impressed with the way those paratroopers were moving on their way out of there.

We were on that fire for four or five more days and we ran out of food up there. We had a lot of big hungry loggers to feed. We had been waiting for a plane to bring us some food and when it did it dropped the food way down by the lake. There was an Assistant Ranger there who said we would have to go down and get it. It was the end of the day and getting dark and it wasn't easy, but we got the packer to get the mules ready and fix them up with the packs. Then he said, "Jimmy, are you going with me?" and I said, "Yeah," because I wasn't going to let anybody beat me and I was going to show that guy that I was just as tough as he was.

We took off down to the lake with the pack string and the packer who was just a little guy. We got to the food all right and got it packed up, but by the time we got back to camp we had been gone all day and all that night and it was close to morning again. I was tired, but not about to give up. As we were finally nearing the fire – I forget the other fellow's name but he was a big, rough individual and I wasn't going to let him beat me – he said, "You know, Jimmy, I've had it, I'm really tired out." I said, "Well, I'm glad you said that because I wasn't going to let you get the best of me." I was all shot myself, with no more fight in me, but we had to get that food in because a lot of the loggers had threatened to walk off the job, because if there is nothing to eat you don't have enough energy to work.

I stayed on that fire about a week and one day Harold said, "Let's hike out and go home, Jim." So we started out on what was a twenty mile hike up the Big Chilliwack to Hannigan Pass and down into Glacier. One good thing I learned from Harold Engles was that when you're out hiking and you come to a creek, have a towel or something with you, take off your shoes and socks and soak your feet in the icy cold water for awhile. Then dry them real good and it will revive you and make your feet feel like new. We made it out to the road in a couple of days and I got home. That was one fire that I will never forget!

1945 was a pretty dry year and I had been doing the same work that I usually did, cruising timber, working on trails, planting trees, etc., etc. – you name it – just about everything you can think of. Along about September Harold Engles called me and told me to go to a fire up on Sloan Creek. A lightning strike had left a fire way up in the top of the hills on a ridge there and he already had the Guard, Floyd Johnson, and two other men up there, but he wanted me to go up and take over. He told me how to get there.

The crew had gone up Sloan Creek towards Cadet Creek about a mile and a half and then had cut straight up over the mountain. It was about two or three miles to the very top and this fire happened to be on a ridge at the very top. So, I took the fire pack and headed out. Once I got up the trail and found where it was taking off I headed straight up the mountain until I found the fire. Floyd had two or three men in there trying to clean it up. There was only about eight acres burning, but it was scattered all over the place, as the lightning had hit it and it had spread to different places, but wasn't burning hard.

I had no communication to the crew below yet. They sent about eight people from the road crew up. The road crew people weren't trained in fighting fires, but we were short on manpower and had to use some of them. Some of them did not like fighting fire because they figured they weren't trained for it, but we had no choice. There was one young fellow who just kept on harping all the time saying he wasn't feeling well, that he had a hurt back and everything else, and everything was wrong. Well, I wrote a note to Harold telling him to keep that fellow in camp as he wasn't going to do me any good keeping on complaining about how bad it was. I was afraid it would affect the other men.

I gave the note to the boy to give to Harold and told him I needed some kind of communication – a radio or something – in order to get a call out. It wasn't too long before Jack Swilling hiked in with a radio and I could communicate with the rest of the world. It was one of those old time radios, but it worked and I was able to call Harold and tell him I needed food for the crew. I had eight men there mopping up and gave him a report on that. I also told him about the young man I had sent down there. I didn't mean to get him fired, but Harold gave him a talking to and he went home. I don't know if he came back and kept working or not, but Harold didn't have a lot of patience with people like that.

Anyway, I told Harold that we needed food for ten of us for about eight days or so, as I didn't know exactly how long we'd be there. He contacted a pilot in Bellingham and they put a packet of grub in the plane and dropped it to us.

I had the men take a pole and shred it and then go into the fire area looking for any sparks which they were to put out and clean up. There was this one guy, whose name I don't remember, who was an easygoing, hard working man. I assigned him the job of taking a five gallon pack and walking way down over a meadow below to get water for the mop up. This wasn't an easy task and so we had to use the water very sparingly. He made several trips down for water and the men worked pretty hard so it wasn't long and we had it mopped up. This wasn't too bad since the fire wasn't spreading.

He served as water carrier for a few days and he did a real good job, but the next time I asked him to get the water he said, "Jimmy, I'm completely worn out – can't you get somebody else to do it?" So I said, "Yes, o.k. you stay in camp here and help the cook or whatever and mop up. But, rest up a little while Floyd and I go down after the water."

I knew I couldn't pack that water by myself so Floyd Johnson and I took the water can down together. Floyd was a big, heavy set fellow and nice to talk to. He'd been in the Army and in places I had never heard of before. He'd been through it all and was quite a drinker too, but up there he couldn't get it. We went on down and got a pack of water and then started back up the hillside. There were lots of wild-flowers blooming – beautiful flowers – and we would sit down and rest.

I remember one time we sat down in a little meadow where there were lots of wildflowers and the bees were thick. A bumblebee landed on a flower right by us and I flipped this great big 'ol bumblebee and it hit him right square in the belly button. He flew up in the air about five feet and his eyes bulged out. Boy did he give me a scolding – he could have killed me! I still laugh about it – it was a temptation I just couldn't resist. I'll never forget how shocked he was or how his eyes bulged out. I don't think the bee even stung him, but it scared the living daylights out of him.

Every day we had to make at least two trips down for water and believe me as hard as that was, we had to use it very sparingly. We would bring one can up in the morning for breakfast for the cooks and all that and the other can was used for what we called "mopping up."

After three or four days I called the Ranger Station and said, "Harold, I've just about got this fire out and there is very little work left on it. I'm going to start sending the men out two at a time until they are all out. I'll send Floyd out with the last bunch and I'll stay here." But, Harold said, "No, you don't stay there – I need you down here. You can leave Floyd in charge and he can send the men out two at a time and he can be the last one out."

As I was leaving there Floyd, who normally stayed down at the cabin at the Guard Station at Sloan Creek (it was a large cabin and a family could live in it) said, "Jimmy, when you get to the cabin lay down on my bed and if you stick your hand under it you'll feel a jug of wine. You should take a swallow or two of it." Well, I never was much of a drinker and so when I got down to the cabin I never even thought of it. I got the phone and called Harold to tell him that I was down at base camp and I would need transportation. He called back and said it would be awhile before he could get anyone up there.

So I lay down on the bed and I flipped over and sure enough I felt that jug of wine and thought, "What the heck, I'll take a few swal-lows." So I poured about a half or three quarters of a glass of wine for myself. I wasn't used to drinking and I didn't know what percent alcohol it was, so I took a swallow of it which made me feel pretty good there for awhile. I waited for some time before Harold came up after me and he said, "Jimmy, where did you get the wine?" and he smiled. I said, "It belongs to Floyd – he has a whole jug of it under his bed." To that Harold said, "We knew we couldn't keep him from having it." That was a little experience that I won't forget.

I want to mention something about the men on this fire. After I got on this fire they sent up a road crew which consisted of fellows who weren't used to hiking. I remember one young man got within hollering distance of the top and said he just couldn't make it any further, that he was going to stay right there even if he had to sleep there. The rest of the crew got to the top and tried to urge him on from there. One guy said, "You had better look around because you are sitting right in the middle of a bees nest." Sure enough, the bees were swarming around him like everything. I never saw a man move so fast – he completely forgot how tired he was and came up that ridge just a-running. He said, "I don't know where I got that energy, but when someone hollered "bees" I moved."

One thing I want to mention is that in the early days of 1946 and 1947 they did clearcutting. They would log a unit completely – taking everything. They had also done some selective logging, but a clearcut is a unit of maybe forty acres entirely cut down. After the timber is removed there is a lot of slash and brush left behind. The Forest Service had to burn that slash in order to have clear ground to plant new trees. It was a dirty job that had to be done.

The whole crew would get together, including the Ranger, and together we would make a plan as to how to burn it. First to be considered was where it laid, east slope or west slope, or whatever and then figure out the prevailing winds, how they blew and how they would affect our fire without backfiring our slash burning. Then we would have to have a Cat or something that would make a trail all around the unit. We had these little torches containing a gas and oil mixture to make them burn good and wicks of wire and wick material. We would get the torches burning and then go around and let them drip on the brush we wanted to burn.

It was important that we wait until the time was just right. We usually watched and waited to determine exactly what the weather was going to do. The best time to light off the slash was just before a rain or when a good dew was coming on and then get it burned before it got too wet.

Once in awhile we'd miss our calculations and the fire would cross the line a little bit, then we would have to get our fire trucks up there and put it out. We would get up on the side of a hill a little ways and start back about fifty feet below the fire trail and burn that cut so that the draft wouldn't take it too fast. We had to watch it because sometimes those fires make their own draft and get carried away. We had to set the fires just right so that we wouldn't burn too much. This could take us several hours because we had to wait until one fire died down completely before we could back down the hill and begin another section. It could take an entire day to burn one whole unit. It was quite interesting work for us and I kind of enjoyed it.

They are not allowed to use this method for burning slash any longer. Now they use skyline equipment and a big rake and put all the slash up in piles to burn it. This is a much better method, even though it costs more, it does a cleaner job with less risk of the fires spreading.

Chapter XVI

One of the reasons the Forest Service was very good to work for was because it had good employee benefits. You earned two days a month annual leave and a half a day a month sick leave. I mention this because one day I thought that maybe I should go down below and look for a job because of the war. The Ranger said I could do what I wanted, but pointed out that while they didn't pay high wages that once a person was on Civil Service and well established there was a good retirement plan. If you spent thirty years there you could draw two-thirds of your salary and retire at age fifty-five or sixty. So I just decided to stay with the Forest Service.

Most of the summer of 1945 I was Headquarters Guard and my job was checking fire boxes in the logging camps and keeping watch over the campgrounds and fire equipment. In the winter I cruised timber and helped lay out sales . . . the usual things that a forest service person does. In 1946 during the summer I was doing the same – working on the trails, cruising timber and doing whatever needed to be done. That fall we had real dry weather.

When a lightning storm goes through the forest it starts fires and hits old snags etc., and in most cases goes straight down to the ground. Usually there is a layer of duff which could consist of pine cones, fir cones and needles, branches, etc., which have fallen on the forest floor over the years and in places this organic matter can be as much as two feet thick. The decomposing forest material makes fertilizer, you might say, for the trees growth. As I said, it is often two feet thick and if a fire gets down into that duff it can smolder for a long time . . . That is what the Forest Service calls a "sleeper."

When a lightning storm passes over there is usually a little rain, but the rain doesn't last long, and that sleeper will stay in there until there is a change in the weather and then it will flare up, start burning and put up some smoke. The lookout person, in a high Lookout may see that smoke through the timber. With his firefinding equipment he can pinpoint that fire to within about 40 acres and tell exactly where it is.

One year a lightning storm hit somewhere up in the South Branch of the North Fork of the Stillaguamish. It might have been in September when it happened and someone reported it to the office. Nels Bruseth called me in and said, "Yimmy, you are going to have to take a couple of men in and try to find that fire and put it out. It's in heavy timber and it has warmed up in there for awhile so you are going to have trouble. Take Byard Tucker and Jack Swilling with you and put on the fire packs. You'll have to go up to Texas Pond and down on the old trail and cross the Stillaguamish, and then from there you can get up on the ridge."

So I got hold of Byard and Jack and we took off the next morning headed out to look for that fire. We hiked for six or seven hours when we found this old trail and tried to guess by the map just about where it was. We followed it on up to the top of the ridge and put our packs down to have a look around. Jack suggested, "Let's go up the trail a little and see if we can find it." So, we headed north on the ridge and pretty soon someone said, "I smell smoke somewhere." We followed the smell of the smoke and sure enough, there was a great big old tall snag, about six or seven feet thick and and the smoke was coming out of it.

Byard said, "Well, we've found it so we'll have to go back and get our packs and come up and make our camp here." So we did that. I said, "We're going to have to get out our crosscut saw and fall that thing and that will take us a day or so." Jack said, "I don't think we'll have to fall that tree, I think it will just burn off." I said, "Jack, that's an awful big tree and that thing will never burn off." He said, "Well, let's wait for fifteen or twenty minutes." And sure enough, in about fifteen or twenty minutes that big old snag just fell down . . . and Jack was so proud . . . That really tickled him.

Jack Swilling was an individual who was a pleasure to be out with because he would tell you stories and make you feel good. He would always have something to tell you about Texas. I liked working with Jack and Byard and they were very good friends of mine. I remember saying I thought we should take a crosscut saw and cut that old snag open or something. We figured we should make camp right there that night, up close to the burning snag so we could keep an eye on it. We had to make our way back to where we left our packs and get them and then get back to where the fire was and set up camp.

Now I'm going to tell you what a "fireman's pack" is, something they don't have anymore. A fireman's pack usually contained a cross-cut saw and a "Pulaski" – or a three-man crew would have one man carry the crosscut saw, the second carry the Pulaski and the third man maybe an axe. Three men would be able to carry the tools to put out a fire. They would also have sleeping bags, first aid kits and K rations.

A K ration was Army food that was put in a pack, each pack containing enough food for one meal. For breakfast there would be corn flakes, powdered milk, a candy bar, a can of fruit, a piece of bread and some kind of juice to drink, and three cigarettes. In those days each meal had three cigarettes in it. The dinners were similar but there would be a can of pork and beans, beef stew, or something like that in place of the corn flakes. Each of us would have enough packages to last three days.

Back at our campsite we opened up our packs to eat our dinner. We were talking and joking when someone said that the only way to get a fire out that was way up inside of a cedar snag was to cut a hole in the top of it. This snag was lying down so we went to the top of it and cut a chunk out of it with the crosscut saw and, sure enough, the fire just poured out of it. Someone said, "We'll never get it out this way." Jack replied, "Well, let's just let it burn up." So we fixed it so there would be a good draft and we just let it burn.

We ate our dinner and fixed up our camp, getting ready to sleep for the night, not knowing for sure what the following day was going to hold for us. I was very uncomfortable there and I was cold. There was some hot stuff close to me and so I moved my sleeping bag over and crawled underneath a log with it and fixed a very comfortable place and rested the rest of the night.

Jack and Byard didn't know what I had done and when they got up in the morning and saw I wasn't there they began to get worried and wondered, "What had become of Jimmy." They couldn't figure out where I had gone and they thought that maybe I had gone crazy and wandered off into the night or something. They stood on the log and hollered and hollered like everything and there I was, right at their feet under the log the whole time. I reached up and grabbed one of them by a foot and it really shook 'em up.

The three of us worked on that fire all day, cutting that snag up into pieces and burning it. We dug a trench all around it so that if it did burn some more, it wouldn't go any farther. We worked for two or three days on that one snag fire. I wanted to tell you about that particular fire because it is typical of what Forest Service men call "smoke chasing." There are lots of them!

While I'm telling this story I want to mention that in 1945 there were so many lightning strikes up in the Suiattle – there were 125 in the Suiattle alone – and there was no way the Forest Service could keep up with all of those fires. So they just hired the people they could to put out the worst fires and the rest of them just had to burn out.

Now, while I'm on this subject I might as well say that the forest sometimes gets very dry.

I also want to say something about the fire at Yellowstone, since that's what happened there many years ago. It got so dry year after year that the trees got old and ripe and they weren't cut for logs, then the lightning struck up in the east and started burning. The environmentalists didn't believe in putting out fires as they thought this was the natural way, and so that fire burned up thousands of acres of good timber that could have been used to build homes. Instead of saving them they let it burn, and I was ashamed of them.

To me this was a very poor way of doing it and it wasn't the way the good Lord meant for us to do with our forests. He left the forests for us to take care of and use for building homes or whatever we needed it for. He wanted us to manage it and we are doing a very poor job of it.

Here in the Northwest someday the weather is going to get real warm, real warm, and the timber is going to get old and over-ripe. Then we're going to get a lightning storm that won't quit and we are going to lose millions and millions of board feet of timber that could make homes. I am just warning you before hand that somebody is going to have to wake up to the fact that we have to do something about the timber. We have to cut it and get it out of there and replace it with fir.

There is another thing that should be remembered, too ... Nowadays you can plant trees and you can put fertilizer in a pill, something like "Miracle Grow" which will make them shoot right up and we will have a perpetual supply of timber. On this I had to have my say!

Anyhow, when Jack and Byard and I got through with that fire we came on down the ridge on the South Bank and came right out where they were building a road at the Twin Bridge. We made it back to Darrington where we reported to Nels that the fire was out. He said, "How did you do it?" We explained to him that it was a big snag that was burning and we just cut it open and burned it up because there wasn't water there to fight it any other way.

Chapter XVII

To begin this chapter I want to give you a description of a typical Ranger Station of the 1940's, describing the personnel and their duties. First there was the Ranger who is usually a well trained man who has been with the Forest Service for a long time. Harold Engles was the Ranger when I was there. He was 14 years older than I and a wonderful person . . . everyone thought the world of Harold and he did much good for the people around him. He was more considerate of his people than any boss I have ever known. As far as I am concerned he rides tall in the saddle. Harold passed away a few years ago at the age of 90.

The next person, the Assistant Ranger, was Nels Bruseth who did the work of lining up fire crews, trail crews and anything pertaining thereto. Nels was a self-educated man who knew music and could play various instruments. He had studied Botany to the point where he could pick up about any plant and tell you about it, he also knew a lot of Indian Lore. He was a promoter and was the person who started the Darrington Volunteer Fire Department. Nels also helped to get the city started and find the first Mayor. He was instrumental in organizing the Timber Bowl Celebrations that we have – I believe the first one was in 1946.

The next person on the staff was Joe Hollingsworth who was an old fellow who had been a logger all of his life and who was a very careful, deliberate person who know what he was doing when there were problems out in the District. He carried food to the different Guard Stations and Lookouts and took letters and equipment to places like Sloan Creek and Bedal campground and Lookouts at French Creek and Whitechuck.

The next person was the Timber Sales Officer, Verne Hicks, and his job was to lay out all the timber sales. The District at that time sold about eighty million board feet a year with the big logging outfit then being the Sauk River Co. who were logging up the Sauk River and who cut most of the timber in that region. We had other smaller outfits like Walt Robinson, Jack Faucett and Floyd Wright and a lot of others that cut two or three hundred thousand board feet a year. Verne's job was to see that everything was the way the contract specified.

Then we had the Fire Crew, the Trail Crew and the Suppression Crew handled by Art Ryals. It had a lot of young fellows in it and I recall only a few of them. There was Walt Robinson, Bud Swilling and his brother and about twenty others in the crew. They worked on trails and maintained the campgrounds, etc. and were the suppression fire crew. They stayed close to the Ranger Station so if there was a fire they would be ready to go right to it.

Jack Swilling was the guard up at the station and I was the Headquarters Guard. Bob Mealy was the crew chief. I worked for him in the summertime and he was a wonderful friend. In fact all of these people were very close friends of mine and we were like one big family – a different type of people than work there now.

About seven of us ran the Ranger Station. We also had a road crew and Ray Bennett was in charge of that. He had a road grader and a backhoe to take care of about fifty miles of gravel roads back into the mountains – one going up the Suiattle and the main Sauk road and one going up the Whitechuck. Ray used the equipment for the entire Mount Baker

Joe Hollingsworth ~ 1944

area and he was transferred around the area. He may have had four or five men working for him.

That pretty well describes the Ranger Station from 1946 to 1951. My job was cruising timber, working on trails, planting trees and all the miscellaneous work that needed to be done. Bob Mealy, one of my best friends, was made a Ranger and transferred down to Oregon which hurt me quite a bit because we worked so well together and we enjoyed it so much, maybe because each of us had a good sense of humor. I like anyone who has a sense of humor.

It was about this time the funds for the Forest Service were getting low and we were going to be laid off for the winter. One day in the fall, Harold Engles and all of us were out planting trees. I hated that job! It was one job I just didn't like to do, so I asked Harold if there was any job he had that I could do other than planting trees.

He said, "Jimmy, if there was a better job in the Forest Service, as the Ranger I would have first choice of it and there just isn't any better job." So I told him that I would like to take a leave of absence to work somewhere else because I had a family to take care of and I needed to work the year around and I asked him if it would be hard to do that. He said, "If you want to take a leave of absence to work somewhere else you can do that, and when you come back you will always be welcome and there will be a job here for you."

So I took a leave of absence from the Forest Service and started working in a shingle mill. I worked there about a year and then I got a job with the school district. I didn't enjoy that job very much as it was driving the school bus and being a bus mechanic. It was tedious work! I didn't like it because my heart was always up in the mountains or in the woods with the Forest Service. I hauled kids to ball games and I didn't make much money – just about enough to make a living. I don't have too much to say about that job.

I did have good people to work with at the school though. Harry Edwards, the Superintendent, was a real nice guy and they were all nice people, my heart just wasn't in that job. I had too much responsibility and very little pay. I stayed on there for awhile and did some surveying on the side with John Newman – just evening and weekend jobs, surveying lots, etc. I held down this job while building a house at Whitehorse.

Then in 1958 the Forest Service began to get a little more money to work with and they had an engineering crew. I was pretty good at that kind of work. I asked Harold Engles if he would hire me back. He said, "Well, Jimmy, I promised you a job any time you wanted to come back to work and you can have the job if you want it, but I'm telling you that you won't enjoy it, as it just isn't like it used to be. A lot of it is just office work and the people are a little different, not the kind you can get close to. They're all trying to make their way up the ladder and too interested in that. You'll just be a number to them."

So at that time I went back to work for the Forest Service in the engineering department. I worked for Al Frizell, who worked out of Bellingham. We surveyed roads with a compass, drew them up, figured out the earthwork and designed them in the wintertime, and then in the summertime the road crews would build them. I was a road inspector for the Forest Service for three or four years. My job was going out to see that the contractor was building the right kind of road and doing it up to the contract specifications.

It was quite a job and I enjoyed it in a way, but all the people weren't easy for me to get along with, as they were all trying to move up the ladder. I wanted to put in the next twenty years here so I went along with them. I met different people and there were a lot of good people there that I worked for, but I don't remember all of their names. My engineering boss was a pretty nice fellow and we got along just fine with me as a road inspector.

I wasn't so much on English and writing and so forth, so was lucky the forms I had to work with were mostly just checkout forms. I just went along and if I found a culvert was in wrong I just checked it out on the sheet of paper and turned it in. I had to keep tabs of everything – if they were on grade and had the right thickness of gravel i.e., fine gravel and coarse gravel, until they got the thing up to snuff, the brush all cut and the culverts in all the right places. It was a big job!

One of the jobs I liked in the Forest Service in engineering was locating new roads because, as I mentioned before, you go out to a patch of timber and lay out new roads from the top to the bottom. One time Harold Engles wanted me to locate a road near the top of Gold Hill where there was a patch of old growth. He wanted me to find it and lay out a 7% grade down to the road. So I got up in the morning, took my lunch and my pack and started up from the bottom of the mountain. I hiked for maybe five or six hours to get to top. While I was there I set my instrument for a 7% adverse grade and I walked and I stepped on this one big log and a coyote or half wolf ran by me. I didn't pay attention to it until I looked up and saw he was growling at me, and his eyes, which were slanted, gave me a little bit of a chill because I knew right then that I was up against something that I didn't expect to see – it was something like a cross between a coyote and a wolf because he looked meaner than a coyote and was frothing at the mouth.

I had a hatchet on my belt and as a Boy Scout I was always good at throwing the hatchet, usually being able to hit my mark every time. My thought was that I would pull the hatchet out and throw it at him, thinking I'd get him right between the eyes. Then I thought that maybe I'd better not as there was a chance I might miss and if I did then I would have no weapon. For some reason I glanced down at my feet and there was a rock. I picked up that rock and threw it and hit the animal right on the side of the head. It didn't seem to hurt him too much, but it made him stop and looked at me for awhile before he turned and slowly walked away. For that I was pretty relieved because I thought if he comes back after me I'll at least have my hatchet. I believe he knew when that rock hit him I wasn't something he wanted to try and make dinner out of.

It was time to get back to work, so I set my Adney at 7% adverse grade and as I went down I threw in a couple of switchbacks. It was about a four mile road that I laid in and it came out at what they call The Four Mile on the Sauk Road. That was one experience with animals in the woods that I won't ever forget.

The first five or six years after I came back to work for the Forest Service they made me a road inspector and I performed the aforementioned duties. You had to know a little bit about engineering, a little bit about culverts and grade the road according to what the contract called for. Most contracts called for a road about eighteen feet wide and the first coat of gravel had to be a coarse coat that ran about a 3 minus. Then they put a fine coat on top of that which would be about an inch and a half minus and would be a finished grade for a logging road.

The first row would be about five or six inches thick and the next row about six inches thick, then the final coat would be about three inches thick. It had to be rolled in and had to be the right grade, also the ditches had to be just so and the culverts were very important. You had to be able to lay those culverts in so they would be in kind of a shingle fashion. Each culvert was made out of galvanized steel or aluminum. Aluminum was best because it was light, although we tried different types of culverts in the ditches.

At that time we had about four outfits that were building roads. Most of the workers were loggers and not big contractors. Some of them I remember were Jack Faucett and his crew, Walt Robinson who hired out some of his road building, and Sam Forrester who had a crew also. One of our largest road builders was the Summit Timber Co. which had a large crew and built a lot of the roads. It really kept you hopping sometimes to get out there and check on them.

There were times when they had to take a break from the road building and grading when conditions were such that too much mud was getting into the streams. We had to be careful not to let this happen as it can cause serious pollution problems for the fish, etc. in the streams. The job was demanding, but I rather liked it in a way. I had a lot of friends out there that I had to be careful about being too good to. An inspector can find himself in trouble if he overlooks something or they think he has been going easy on his buddies.

Before the road inspector job, when I was surveying, we had a survey crew that we took way back up into Sloan Creek. We went up

Sloan Creek about three or four miles and then crossed it coming back down the other way. It was about five or six miles of it up there and we could work a lot of that road by surveying from the Sloan Creek cabin.

When we surveyed we used a compass to get the bearings, etc. and then we measured off the distance and put in what they called a grade stake wherever the ground changed in topography. This stake would mark the height and then we'd come back and run levels at each one of those points, high or low, and note it in the level book. With this information we were able to take side casts and get the topography of the slope on each side of the proposed road.

We would work in the office in the wintertime and draw these up, getting what you call the earthwork on it – how much soil was to be moved one way or the other – also having to classify the soil. However, I'm getting ahead of myself because that was done later.

One time there were three or for of us sent way up Sloan Creek to do some surveying. Al Frizell was the road locator at that time, and he was a good one. He could go out and locate where the road would have to be built to most easily reach a particular patch of timber. Anyway he located this road way up Sloan Creek, and I don't remember if he had a plane drop our supplies or not, but we had a camp up there one time and stayed there while we worked. We couldn't walk in and out of there everyday because it was too far to hike.

There was Joe Ensley, myself, Don MacBay and one other fellow whose name I can't remember. Don MacBay was in charge and I was new back then, and not very well known. If I hadn't taken leave and had stayed with the Forest Service I would have been up there a little higher, but I wasn't. Joe Ensley had worked with me before. He was a lot younger than myself, in fact he had graduated from high school with my daughter. Anyway, when we made camp we found out that everything was fir and we had an awful lot of mice around.

I didn't know there were so many mice out in the woods. They were called field mice and they were just thick. We couldn't seem to put our lunches anywhere that they couldn't get into. We had to put them in a can or something to keep them out. One boy said, "Well, I'll fix them," so he put his lunch in a paper sack and he walked out on a little island that was in a creek and hung his lunch on a tree limb hanging over the creek. He stood back and said, "Now, let's see if they can get that." Sure enough, the mice got across the creek, climbed up the tree, out on the branch and down the string to get to his lunch. We though that was amazing!

We finally solved the problem by getting a five gallon can with a hard lid on it and we kept our lunches in that. One night we decided to see who could catch the most mice. We took a milk can and put a hole right through the center of it then ran a stick through it and filled the 5 gallon can half full of water. We'd lay the stick across the top so that when a mouse jumped on the can it would turn. We put a piece of cheese on it and would see who would catch the most mice. I think the record caught in one day was twenty-seven mice.

One morning while we were having breakfast Joe was in charge of frying the hotcakes. MacBay and I already had ours and Joe was just laying his out along with some eggs. He had a can of syrup lying there that he had forgotten to close. Without even thinking about it he started putting syrup on his hot cakes and a mouse's tail stuck out of the can opening. I could have thrown up, but it was too late because my food had gone down all right. It made Joe a little bit sick so he threw the syrup away and threw his hot cakes away too. I'll never forget that. Joe said, "Don't tell MacBay," because he was the kind who would really get sick over a thing like that.

We were there for a couple of weeks, off and on. Joe Ensley was an expert fisherman and he would go out about every day and catch fish for our breakfast. They were all about seven or eight inch fish. The secret to his success was that one day he would go to one pool and catch eight or nine fish, but the next day he'd skip that pool and go to the next one, always keeping one ahead of the other. I figure those fish must have come from up at Johnson Lake.

This is a story that I want to get in here. Someone asked me if I had ever been lost in the woods. Well, one day I was told to go up on top of Gold Hill and run down some old mining claims that had been put up there in 1910, owned by different people, they were what you call patent mines. A mine is usually 660 feet wide and 990 feet long and runs with the length of the mountain. Most people who patented them would patent every other claim which would tie the one up in the middle. One person could only patent one mine at a time. Anyway, I was told to go and try to find some of the old markers. So I took off and headed straight on up to the top.

Most people think that Gold Hill has a sharp ridge at the top. There is one spot that has a sharp ridge. I kept going towards the south about as far as you can on the ridge and came to a big flat. It was a day with no sun, but warm, foggy and cloudy. The sun never did come out! I got to walking around in there and then decided I had to go and tend to my business. I took my cruiser's jacket that I always carried with me. In that jacket I always had a compass, a knife, my lunch and a first aid kit . . . I carried quite a lot of equipment in case I was caught out overnight.

This time I'd foolishly hung my jacket on a banch and went over to the creek. It was so flat in that area that the creek ran in switchbacks as it flowed through the woods. It was an interesting area and I always had the habit of looking the country over and putting different things in my mind, picking out landmarks like old snags and maybe some rock outcrop or some unfamiliar tree . . . something I wasn't likely to forget. I got to wandering and started up the creek for some reason because something was a little more interesting there and I just kept going. Finally I decided I better head back and get my jacket. First thing, to my dismay, I turned around a few times and I was lost. I just didn't know what to do as I had never felt that way before.

I had been mixed up in the woods a lot of times, but I didn't ever figure that I was lost. But this time I was lost! I couldn't hear any whistles or horns or any noise whatsoever. I almost panicked! I looked up because I'd always been told that all the tops of the trees in this country bend kind of to the northeast. The prevailing winds are from the southwest and it forces the tops of all these trees to bend to the northeast. I looked up and sure enough I found that all the tree tops were bending northeast and so I knew what the directions were from there, but then I couldn't figure out from which direction I had come.

I thought maybe I'd just come up the creek and I must have been lost for maybe an hour or more before I began to get worried. It was starting to get a little late and I should have eaten my lunch by now and been back to work. So I followed the stream on down and finally came to where I saw my jacket hanging on a branch. I could hardly believe my eyes when I saw that jacket, but I felt so relieved that I put it in my mind that, "never again would I take my jacket off and leave it anywhere like that." I always remember that experience because it was the only time that it bothered me to get lost.

Like I said, I had been mixed up plenty of times before, but I always had a good idea where I was and so it was no big deal. This time I just didn't know how I was going to get out. I included this story to make the point to people that no matter how good a woodsman you are you can get mixed up and lost, therefore you must have the right stuff with you at all times.

Chapter XVIII

This chapter is about cabins which are quite fascinating. There are many different types and names for them. One of the longest names that sticks in my mind is the one called the Adirondack Shelter. It is a shelter that is built with three sides, a log back and log sides, although some were built out of cedar shakes. They always have a overhang up front, plus a roof – a little small roof up in the front. They built them for a place to camp in, and you could build your fire out in front of the cabin so instead of having a big tent you just had a pleasant little cabin.

I want to tell a story about a cabin that I ran across years ago. One time Harold Engles sent me to work with a couple of logging engineers from the Sauk River Co. Sauk River, in the early forties, had a camp up at the Whitechuck. Harold said, "Jimmy, I want you to go up there and work with Mack and Gus." (That's all I can remember of their names.)

Mack was a logging engineer and was an older man in his sixties. Harold said I could learn something from these two. Being an old logging engineer, Mack knew how to pace. He could pace up to one hundred feet and hit it right on the nose. He would go very slowly and carefully and I'd follow along beside him. The purpose of this was to figure an approximate size and amount of timber in a certain area, and to get an idea what the cost of logging and getting it out would be. He then reported this information to Jamison, the owner of the Sauk River Mill Co.

One time we were working way up beyond Conn Creek, a tributary of the Sauk River. We were up at the headwaters of it in the trees way up near the top. Very few people had been up there for a long long time. Old Mack was way down in front of me one day pacing, and I'm not sure where Gus was at the time. I looked way down the hill where the timber was pretty well open and I could see a cabin. So I called to

Mack and asked if we were anywhere near a logging camp and he said, "No." So I asked if there were supposed to be any cabins around and he said, "No." So I said, "Well, there's one way down there." So he took his foot and very carefully marked the spot where he left off so that he could continue and said, "Come on Jimmy, let's go down and investigate."

We knew there hadn't been anyone in there for a few years and were surprised to find what a beautiful cabin it was. It was very old, having probably been built during World War I or when it was first over. The old man who built it had taken cedar logs and split them and dove-tailed each one on all four sides. The timbers on the roof hung way over so that he had a nice shelter out front and he had split cedar into diamond shape strips and pounded them in between the logs rather than putting moss in the cracks to seal 'em up real good. There was a fireplace inside the cabin and in front of the fireplace there was an old cooker of some kind. It was an unusual wire contraption, with wires twisted this way and that so a biscuit pan, etc. could be set on it. It was a good sized cabin, about 12' x 18', well built and very beautiful.

In one corner of the cabin I found an old crosscut saw he had greased before leaving and some homemade snowshoes made out of vine maple. Vine maple is good for that. He'd spun it and twisted it around and put leather thongs all through it so it wouldn't sink. But the mice had gotten up where he had hung them and had chewed the strips all up. Anyway, we looked all around and at the time I thought to myself, "I have to remember where this is." It was really something!

The cabin was built right next to the headwaters of a little stream that is a tributary of Conn Creek, which runs down into the Sauk River which in turn flows into the Skagit River. To go on with the story about the cabin, I took well note of it, where it was, and we left and we finished up that day and when I got to the Ranger Station that night, Nels Bruseth, an old timer who had been there for many years, was in the office. I told him that I had found a cedar plaque at the cabin that said, "Mr. Strom" on it and "1924". So I was telling Nels about finding the cabin way up Conn Creek with the sign and he got all excited. He said he used to know where it was, but had lost that cabin and had been wondering about it for years. He said he would like to go up and see it.

I asked him what the story was with that cabin? "Well," he said, "there was a fellow by the name of Conn who came up here right after the war was over who didn't want to do anything except trap and prospect. He had a lot of money and a lot of time, and that's when he built the cabin." So I asked how Strom's name got on it? He said, "Strom was a Norwegian who helped build the gold mines on the side of the hill and he was also a prospector. The other prospectors didn't trust him and they didn't like him because they figured he was the one who had shot a man or killed a man up on Asbestos Creek over a mining claim. His body had drifted down there and that was why they called it 'Skull Creek' for awhile."

But to go on with the story, Conn hated old Strom and told him that if he ever caught him around his cabin he would kill him. After Mr. Conn died Strom got in there and took possession of the cabin. Anyway Nels said we would go up and take a look at the cabin. Years later when Harold Engles had me working on timber sales doing cruising and laying out sales he sent me up there to make a timber sale around that area. I thought that would give me a chance to save that cabin, because when you lay out a sale you take a compass and survey the area by taking angles and drawing lines, etc., then draw it up in the office. So I did that, however the other sales officers, when they got ready to cut the timber, went up and saw my cutting lines and wondered why Jimmy had cut clear around here. They figured that it wasn't right and that it had to be changed. They went down and made a short cut and cut this little circle out (they didn't know that the cabin was in there).

Years later when the Wright brothers, I believe, logged there in about 1948 or 1950, they felled timber and smashed the cabin. I can still see that cabin in my mind's eye.

We always had a lot of those Adirondack lean-tos and other cabins that I'll talk about. There was a cabin way up Clear Creek, an Adirondack lean-to built between Copper Creek and Clear Creek. The trail crews often sayed in there and I stayed there once with the trail crew. Halfway up there at the Four Mile there was another lean-to, but most of those lean-tos were built out of cedar shakes. They were built according to the Adirondack lean-to, but instead of logs they were cedar shakes. There was one cabin that was used a lot and there was another cabin built way up Clear Creek that I am talking about.

There were several cabins up there in the woods and I didn't find them all. I found some of them later. Anyway, there was also a cabin up the Boulder at the Four Mile and they had a lean-to at the Ford where you cross the creek that goes up into Goat Flats. It was also an Adirondack lean-to type cabin. From there we hiked on up to Tupso Pass and from there up to Lake Myrtle and then hiked all the way back to Goat Flats.

There was also a cabin there that belonged to the Guard Station and that one was a regular log cabin with a lean-to on the side of it. Way up in Round Mountain there was a little Pass that goes over the hill. I was there with Nels one time, we called it Coney Pass, and there was a beautiful little Adirondack lean-to up there that was seldom used except by hunters. Then coming on down the hill way up the Stillaguamish there was a lean-to for the C.C.C. boys to use while working on the trail.

Dr. Blake had a lean-to built on the side of North Mountain where he had a timber claim years and years ago when he first came to Darrington. That was what he did. He wasn't a doctor then, but later he went back to study medicine and then returned to Darrington as a doctor. There is a lean-to way up on the side of Prairie Mountain and then if you go way up Sloan Creek where there is a regular cabin, a two room cabin, that was built for the Guard. There was also one at Kennedy Hot Springs for the Guard.

Years later in the late fifties and sixties there were a lot of people called "Hippies" wandering around in the woods who would get into these cabins and live there. They would bring in supplies and then set a canvas up in front of the lean-to and take possession of it. The Forest Service didn't like this because some of them were on drugs. Somehow, I think, an order was given to Slim Welch to burn what he found, the good ones, which angered me at the time, but come to think about it, it was the best thing to do.

Some of the most unique cabins that I ever found were way back in the thirties. Shortly after I was married, a friend of mine from the Navy came up and wanted to go on a fishing trip. We heard of a lake way up Illabot Creek, up the Skagit about eight miles above Concrete and on the right hand side of the river. You go up there over some rough terrain before you come to Illabot Creek, but the Forest Service had a trail back in there. So I and David Stromey and his brother-in-law took off one day to hike back up in there.

When we got to the lake we found a cabin. It was built up against a great big rock slab or cliff and was very well built. They had made it so that the cliff was one end of the cabin and had built the fireplace down below it so when they made a fire in there it slowly heated up that entire rock face. That cabin was so well fixed that the rock kept the cabin warm at night. Sometime since the 1930's a slide came down and destroyed that place, I believe. The story goes that a fellow by the name of Brown, a trapper from Concrete, had built the cabin and he told the Sheriff and others that he was going back in there to trap and that if he didn't come out by March to send someone in to look for him.

Well, he wasn't out by March, so they sent someone in to look for him. When they got to the cabin they found all of his equipment there, but it looked as if no one had been there for a long time – his rifles, snowshoes and everything were there – but they never found Mr. Brown. Up in that Illabot Creek country on the side of the hill are deep, deep crevices in the rocks which look as though an earthquake had split them open and left them there. When I dropped a rock in one we could hear it go "tick, tick, tick" clear out of sight. That Mr. Brown just may have fallen into one of those crevices because they never did find him.

Chapter XIX

Now there is something I want to bring up that may be of interest to campers, hunters and fishermen.

One time we got stuck up in the hills and it was real cold. Somehow we had burnt up a cedar snag which had burned all day and we thought, "by gosh, it is awfully warm there" so we pulled all of the hot coals out of that spot and put our sleeping bags where the fire had been and it kept us warm all night long. That rock and soil and all acted as an insulation against the cold.

The way to do this in a lean-to, if you possibly can, is to dig a trench about the size of your body, one for each person. If you are going to be there very long, build your fire in there – get a lot of rocks and put them on the bottom and just build the fire and keep it going good and hot. Then, when evening comes, you let the fire burn out or put it out and put all of the hot coals off to one side. You now have a bed of hot rocks that you can cover with a duffel or something that won't burn and you put your sleeping bag in there and it will keep you warm all night long. We found that out one time when we were camping up on Helena Ridge, and I used that technique a lot when I was camping out.

Another thing I want to mention is camp cooking! Now I did learn one time how to make an "Emmu," that's a camp stove. If you are going to be camping in one spot for several days and you have your campfire going you build it in one spot just like you did for your bed, but you build it out in the open and put lots of rocks in it and keep it going for four or five hours. Then if you have an "Emmu" which consists of a chunk of chicken, venison or meat – or even a leg of lamb – you take that meat and you cut it open and fill it with onions, garlic and anything else you can find.

The first thing you need to do is find an old gunny sack or something like that and lay it on the ground. Then you cover it with sword ferns, a thin layer, and then get some regular lettuce and spread on top of the ferns. Then you put your meat on the lettuce and put asparagus tips, potatoes and carrots around it and salt and pepper it heavily. Roll it up in the cloth like a bundle and wire it or tie it and dip it in the stream to get it soaking wet. Then you take all the hot rocks and soil and everything out of your fire pit and put your Emmu right in there and cover it with all the hot rocks and soil that you just scooped out of the pit.

Now all you have to do is go on a hike or go fishing and come back in three or four hours and dig it up. You will have a very delicious meal, and I mean it is good! We used to do that a lot in the Forest Service.

Chapter XX

I'm going to talk about the Forest Service surveys and how they were done.

The Forest Service wasn't the type that went into first class surveys – you used an old compass. When I was in the C.C.C. camp I learned to use a large compass and chain and an Adney to get elevations. You had to get your elevations and your distance. Anyway, they had the type like George Washington had way back in the early days when he first started surveying.

To go back a little – Between 1889 and 1911 they sent surveyors out of Washington, D.C. and gave them contracts of maybe six hundred dollars per section and those fellows chained it with a chain that was 66 feet long with 100 links in it. It was a mile cut up into portions, you might say, and they would put corners every forty chains or eighty chains apart to make a mile. Then they would go a mile and find a location and they would take a rock and engrave on it the Section Corner and the date and location of this corner (Township, Range and Section) and they did a very good job.

After chiseling the information on the rock they would bury that rock maybe eighteen inches under the ground or it might be sticking up out of the ground. Then they would go to a large tree nearby and engrave on it how far it was over to that corner, how many feet. These trees were called "Witness" trees which were engraved with the description of the corner and the distance to it and would leave it there. That was in 1889 to 1911 and they would do that all through the Forest Service land and then recorded all that information in Washington, D.C.

In order to find those corners you had to get the notes of the original survey and most of that surveying was done with a transit and most of it was quite accurate according to their way. To find those corners you just had to repeat what they did, using the compass and the chain. It was rustic and rough, but all we cared about was being sure we were located on the right spot and not on someone else's property.

We achieved more and more perfection in laying out corners and finally the time came when people began to own property bordering the National Forest and they wanted the Forest Service to survey it. That was my job for the last part of the year. The compasses we used were old fashioned, you might say, and we graduated up to a transit where you had to go into better detail and draw maps. Then they came out with what they called a Theodolite with a computer on it so actually the surveyor didn't have to know too much.

People would come in and say that the Forest Service was on their land and I would go out with the transit and locate the correct lines for them.

Chapter XXI

Sometime around 1962 there was a big fire over in the Lake Chelan area near the town of Chelan, and so they called it the Chelan fire. This fire burned nearly 4,000 acres and they called the Darrington Ranger Station for help, asking us to send over two fire trucks. We had two of them and the first thing I did was to jump in and ask to go. They gave me a nice new fire truck with about a 300 gallon water tank and I was supposed to take a helper with me and go over on that fire.

We had another truck that had about a 200 gallon water tank, a smaller truck that was still in good shape. Danny Ryals was selected to take that truck. He wanted to trade me trucks, but I said, "No way, I'm going to keep this truck right through the fire if I can." He said, "Well, it will give you a lot of trouble because you'll have to work a lot harder with it." I said, "Well, I'll take it." So we went to the fire and we were both working from the same spot.

We would fill the tanks and take a partner with us and drive along the road where the fire had been and put out the spot fires . . . and there were a lot of them. Wherever a fire had cropped up they would send us to get to it and we were there for two or three days before we finally got the lower part of the fire mopped up.

We were a very short distance, about ten miles, from the town of Chelan and in the evening sometimes we would go down there and get some ice cream and take a shower. They had City showers for us to use and public restrooms. The crews always chose me to drive them to town because we had a big crew truck that we could pile a lot of guys in. A lot of them would head for the taverns and do a lot of heavy drinking. I didn't drink or smoke so that was why they chose me to take the truck, so they could get back safely.

Well, one day coming back from town, one of the fellows crawled up in the front of the truck and said he wanted to talk to me, though I couldn't figure out why. He said, "Jimmy, you're a Christian aren't you?" And I said, "Yes, why do you ask that?" He said, "Well, how do you become a Christian?" I said, "Well, all you have to do is accept the Lord as your Savior and don't pay any attention to what you do now, because if you keep praying long enough you'll get out of all your bad habits and get normal. All you have to do is believe in Him and you will be a Christian." I'll always remember that conversation.

I worked on that fire for two or three days and the time came when we had the fire mopped up and they didn't need the big truck there any longer. So they sent me on up the hill and Danny got a big kick out of that saying, "Now do you want to trade trucks with me? If you stayed here you would get to go to town at night and clean up and get dinner in town and that would be much more enjoyable. But, if you go on up the hill there is no way of getting cleaned up and you'll eat in the fire camp, etc."

With that we parted ways and he laughed at me because I had to go up the hill. It wasn't long before I had to come back down to the camp and he was waiting for me and said, "Jimmy, every time I go to town for a shower, I take a shower for myself and I take a shower for you, when I go to the tavern I get a beer for myself and one for you, and when I go to the restaurant I get a nice dinner for myself and one for you and then I get a milkshake for myself and one for you." He'd just sit there and laugh about it. I got a big kick out of that! We were on that fire for some time, as it burned up about 4,000 acres of timber. I'll always remember being with Danny on that fire.

Chapter XXII

This next story will take a little while to tell, but it is one of my most important fire stories – one of the most important times of my life, and I didn't even know it at the time.

About 1963 they had a fire up in a place called the Entiat River on the east side. The fire must have covered about 4,000 acres and was called the Fourth of July fire. The Entiat River runs into a reservoir that's attached to the Rocky Reach Dam which is about 20 miles above Wenatchee and the river runs in about half way up there. In the fall of the year after that fire was out the government began to worry about the material left by the fire since it was right on the river and there were lots of little streams that ran into that river.

They felt a need to rehabilitate the place, as they were worried about the little streams and all the stuff that had fallen into them – chunks and logs, etc. – that maybe in the winter time the creeks would come up and there would be no vegetation or anything to stop them and it would wash all those chunks and logs down into the river and eventually into the reservoir where they might do damage to the turbines of the electric plant.

At that time they sent a bunch of us over there. Bob Ensley and I and one other person were there to handle some crews sent in to clean things up and to make some little coffer dams or little lock dams. We'd take a log and put it across the creek and bury it to stop the soil from washing down too fast. Then we'd pick up all the logs and stuff laying on the edge so they wouldn't wash down. But to come back on the story, they had different crews for different men. When I was there I was probably the oldest man in one of the crews so the Supervisor said they had a special crew for me that no one else wanted to handle.

They had a crew of retarded men who had been working for the town of Wenatchee. I didn't know it at the time, but they were a special group of men that the town of Wenatchee took pride in helping. I didn't want to take that crew on and I told the Supervisor I just couldn't do it because I always thought they were far below the ability to learn anything. He said he would give me a teacher to help me, and said that because he knew I didn't have a temper and could handle things pretty cool he thought I had what it would take to work with this group of men. He said, "It takes someone cool and easy going and I know you can handle them, and we'd sure appreciate it if you would take it over." Well, I said O.K.

There were ten to twenty of these men in the group and I tell you it just made you sick to think how little they did know. I had to take them out and show them a stump. It was a stump where a tree had been felled. They didn't know what a stump was. So I would go over and pat it and say, "This is a stump" and then I'd go over to a log and pat the log and say, "Now, this is a log." It was really hard to get the work out of them and I just had to play along with them which was a very tricky job.

I had to teach them how to whittle up a few shavings to start a fire to burn the logs and trash. They just didn't know which way to move unless you showed them. The way I would do that is I would go up to a log or a chunk that was large and I'd say, "Boy, this thing is heavy, I can't lift it and I have to have someone strong to do it." And they would step right up to show me their strength and then I would praise them and that's the way it worked. You had to like them and you had to praise them and the more you did that the more they thought of you and would look to you as their leader. It was heartwarming and heart tearing and so pitiful.

I remember one day we were pruning brush and I had to send one of the boys up to get some fuel for my torch. The fuel was made out of diesel oil and about 50% or 25% gas. You had to be very careful with it because if you got too much gas in it it would burn or backfire on you and get you into trouble. Anyway, I told this one boy to go up on the road and get me some fuel for my torch in a can. So he went up there and I don't know how he happened to get ahold of gas, but he put gas in the can and brought it down to me. I had already put some in the torch and then I thought maybe I should check it. So I put a little bit on the brush pile and lit it and sure enough, it was gas.

I didn't get mad at him, but turned around and said to him jokingly, "You're trying to get rid of your boss. You brought me gas, do you want to get rid of me and blow me up?" At that he cried! He was so hurt to think I would accuse him of trying to get rid of me. I had an awful time trying to quiet him down. I didn't know they would be so sensitive, but they were.

Each of those men was talented in some special way. Retarded people are God's people – no one will look after them but the good Lord Himself. That was what I thought – they got help from no one and they had no one to take care of them or do their thinking for them. But anyway, each one was a specialist at something.

One boy brought out a radio and would play it and I told him, "If you bring that radio out here you will ruin it." One day I noticed he had the radio on to a song and he was singing it just as perfect and beautiful as it was coming over that radio. It was a beautiful song and he sang it beautifully. But the moment that music stopped he was so illiterate he could hardly talk. Music was his specialty and he made the point to me that he was a musician and loved music and that was his number one thing. Each of them seemed to have some special ability.

I had one boy there who was a pitcher and I didn't find that out until we were down on the road one time and one of the other crew bosses on the other side of the river was skimming snowballs across. It wasn't very wide right there, but he was throwing snowballs at the crew and the foreman was sitting in the truck with the windows rolled down. This kid said to me, "Jimmy, I can put a snowball right in that window if you want me to." I said, "You just roll one up and see." And sure enough he surprised that foreman because it went "WHAM" right into the window. The foreman rolled the window up real fast and brushed the snow off and the rest of the crew kidded him about it. He rolled the window down and said, "You couldn't do that again." The fellow rolled up another snowball and sure enough, put it right through that window again. That was his specialty!

Each one of them had one thing that he could do really well.

I taught one young boy how to whittle shavings and build a fire and he had the impression that that was all he had to do – whittle shavings and build fires. The crew was pretty hard to handle sometimes. I went away one time for a day and they had another crew foreman and they had a fit. He didn't know how to handle them and he had no respect for them because he overemphasized his authority. He tried to make a big deal out of it which didn't work with them. So we kept on doing the rehabilitating work and it got real late in the fall and I just felt worn out or depressed, to the point where it was almost a breakdown handling this crew because I felt so sorry for them.

It was easy to fall in love with these people because I knew that they were God's people – the kind of people the good Lord takes care of day in and day out. I stuck with this job through the winter and I had my wife come over and stay with me for a week which was nice. The government paid for my hotel and my meals and we had it good in a way except the weather was really bad. It was hard work getting up in the morning and going out there with that crew – not so much hard work as it was nerve wracking to do it. We stuck around there until the snow as pretty deep and then I brought the crew down one last time and we were through with it for that year.

I came home that winter, probably in November, because I remember being home for Thanksgiving. Bob Ensley and Joe Ensley were there at the same time because I remember Bob wanted to buy an old drag saw and he found one across the river. He wanted this drag saw for a souvenir because they didn't make them any more.

I'll never forget working with that crew and I was very well praised for it. That year when I got my efficiency rating they really built me up. I found out later that they were watching me and they were watching that crew and they gave them a lot of attention because they really were special. They were special people that you have to take care of and I wasn't expecting it, but they wrote me up a letter that I'll never forget. I felt pretty good about that because they praised me so much for the way I handled that crew when I hadn't realized how much good I had done for them until the end of that year.

Chapter XXIII

About 1970 I was getting up around 55 years old and I could see handwriting on the wall. There was retirement hinted at and new people, a different type of people, in the Forest Service. Conditions were changing and it wasn't the good old Forest Service that I had known before. I knew that retirement was coming up before long.

At the office they kept questioning the shape I was in and they had what they called a step test for people who fight fires. They figured they would make me take that step test and find out I wasn't in good enough condition. But I surprised them! I was in excellent condition.

The test involves taking your heart rate and pulse and then they have you go up and down those steps for four or five minutes and then they take your heart rate, etc. again. Well, my heart beat was about 48 beats per minute which was very slow. So they put me on this step test and hiked me up and down and up and down and my heart rate would only go up to maybe 55 beats per minute. They couldn't understand this because there were fellows there much younger than I who would step on with a heart beat of maybe 52 and theirs would go up to 72. They just couldn't get over that and tried to pull everything they could think of to see just how much I could take.

They decided they would catch me sometime as I was coming in out of the field and give me that step test. So this one day I came in with my cork boots on as I had been up on North Mountain all day working on a road. They were waiting for me and when I came in they wanted me to take that step test. I said, O.K. I'd take it and so I took off my cork boots and they checked my heartbeat which was still around 48. I walked up and down those steps for them and my heart rate only went up to about 56 and they still couldn't get over that. But, I could see that I was going to have to retire before long so I started looking around for a place for retirement.

There happened to be a little place for sale in the southwestern part of Darrington that had a big swamp on it that a couple of fellows owned and used for pack horses. They had four or five horses there that they used to pack people into the mountains on vacation trips. The owners were Dr. Robert Koop and Scoop MacCaully and when they finally decided to give up the packing Scoop wanted to sell the place. Anyway, I bought the place because I could see certain potential there that I could use it for if I retired.

Someone told me one time that I wasn't old for my age and was pretty young yet and I had time to make another career right there. So I gave a lot of thought to this land I had bought and thought about having a trout farm. At that time people thought a trout farm wasn't anything that anybody could make any money at. I wanted a retirement where I could be my own boss and I didn't care if I made any money or not because I had the retirement. So I started the trout farm. I'll tell you more about that as time goes along.

Bobby, my son, and Eleanor, my daughter, came up to visit about that time. Eleanor was living down below and Bobby was just getting ready to go into the Army. They came up and I took them out and showed them the place I had bought and they had a fit, saying, "Daddy, you just bought a big swamp." And they could not figure out what I was going to do with that old swamp. But I had ideas and I was going to work on it.

I had another five years to work in which I did odd jobs, worked on the road inspection crew and with other crews on various jobs for the Forest Service.

In 1972 I had the job of classifying roads and we had forgotten one way up in the North Fork of the Stillaguamish. Ted Hinches who was designing the road said, "You're going to have to go way back up the Stillaguamish and re-classify a road." It was about June and at that time they wouldn't let me go up in the woods by myself anymore because they thought I was too old. So they gave me a helper, Bruce Bryson, to go with me. He went along with me to see that I didn't get hurt.

We were way up at the beginning of the road and I put all of my classifications on tape. I'd walk along the road and say what kind of soil there was and where the culverts had to be put and where the creeks were, etc. I was classifying the road for the designer. We were on our way back down when Bruce looked up in the woods and saw a bear who had a little cub with her. He said, "Jimmy, there's a bear out there with a cub." I told him to think nothing of it as I'd seen hundreds of 'em out in the woods and they never bothered me. He said, "Jimmy, this one is frothing at the mouth and she is coming right down the hill after us." There was an old trail there and I started running down it as fast as I could with Bruce right behind me. I ran so fast I just hurtled right over the top of the old blowdown. I guess I must have run about 300 feet right off the trail into the woods before I turned to see how Bruce was doing, and saw that the bear had gone.

I said, "Bruce, how close did that bear get to you?" He said, "She was nipping at my heels. My heart was beating so fast I could hear it." Bruce asked, "Jimmy, how old are you?" I said, "I'm 56 – why?" He said, "I hope when I get to be 56 years old that I can run as fast as you were." I said, "I suppose you could if a bear was after you."

Chapter XXIV

It was about 1967 when I bought the property to build the fish farm on. I was fifty-one years old and in good health but could see that I was going to have to get out of the Forest Service eventually. The people there were changing and I didn't want any part of it.

I didn't want to retire illiterate so I went to college in the summertime during the next four or five years and planned to do fish farming on the place I had bought. About 1968 I broke ground for my first pond. Bob Cope was logging and that summer they were closed down because of fire season so I had him bring up his equipment. He had a gravel truck and a Cat so he started scooping out that soil. There were a lot of people in Darrington who wanted soil for their gardens because Darrington is nothing but sand, and this was good black bottom soil. I believe I sold it for $1.50 a yard and I can't remember how many yards we hauled out of there.

They were also doing some landscaping at the Forest Service and they needed some soil. Someone asked me if I had some and I said I had some black soil being dug out to make the pond. The Department of Agriculture sent someone out to look and they decided that soil wasn't what they were looking for. However, down by the road they found some land that they said had soil that was exactly what they wanted. It was decomposed pumice rock and it was already innoculated with all of the things needed to grow plants. I had thought all the time that it was sand. They said they would pay me a dollar a yard for that stuff down by the road and I said O.K. I believe they bought about 500 or 5000 yards because I made a little pond in there about 100 feet square. I never thought much about it but I made it into a pond.

Before I had Bob dig the pond I went to the Department of Agriculture to be sure I had a right to do so. They said it would be fine and that they wanted me to build a pond as it would be part of an agricultural project. They came up and made a survey of the grounds and elevations, etc., and they paid me for taking 5000 yards of soil out of there. We took the soil out and piled it to one side and Bob made a lake there about 400 feet long and 200 feet wide. It was a beautiful lake.

We dug it down to about twelve feet and when I felt it was deep enough I had Bob take his Cat and scoop out a spot and we got down there to see if there was water. Sure enough, when we got down there the water just started boiling up. We took a cable and one of the drums and hooked it on to a big maple tree and he winched himself out. He did a wonderful job there. We ran into a little trouble with the County about permits, etc. They kept after me because I had to burn the brush, and they didn't know whether I was in the City or the County.

When I got the lake built I thought it would really be nice to have a little hatchery, so I made some hatchery troughs. I painted them and I set them in the creek and bought a little pump and pumped water through it. Then I went to the Game Department in Arlington to see if I could get some eggs to hatch out in there. The fellow there by the name of Roy Rafton, who was running it, said the State didn't do it

Jimmy Anderson at Trout Farm ~ 1987.

that way. They didn't sell eggs and I would have to go to a private outfit and get the eggs. So I went back home and finally Roy and his supervisor came up and saw my setup and thought it was wonderful.

They had me experiment with about 11,000 hatchery eggs. I was supposed to take those eggs and take any trout that hatched from them and put them up in ponds on the Suiattle and other places and I could keep some for my work. Roy was an awfully good teacher who taught me how to take care of them, how to clean the troughs, how to pick out the rotten eggs and what the temperature of the water should be, etc. He brought me lots of information.

The next thing I had to do for the hatchery was to cement the floor of the barn. The elevation we wanted in the lake was about two or three feet below the floor of the barn. So I had a friend excavate out about four feet of the floor of the barn to make it about seven feet below the elevation of the lake. I cemented that in and made a couple sides. I had a friend of mine from Seattle, Bill, come up and we bought the very best cedar that we could find, 2 x 12's. We dove-tailed and we glued and we made some efficient, good looking, troughs. I built a couple of little concrete piers to set them on top of and I built a couple of little concrete piers to set them on on the inside. I set these two troughs on the piers and I had a pipeline running from the lake down to the hatchery.

I made a nice looking little hatchery where I could put lots of little eggs. I had two raceways built in there which were about 4 x 3 x 24 feet long. After the little fish, called "Alvins", were hatched out and after they got big enough and wore off their little sacs underneath, they were called "flies". When the flies got too big for the troughs I'd put them in my little raceways in the barn and leave them there for awhile.

Then I built a holding pond outside and when they were about three or four inches long I'd put them in the holding pond. I bought eggs from Tacoma Trout Lodge in Tacoma. I would hatch those eggs out, maybe 50,000 of them, and put them in the trough and wait until they got big enough. Then I'd advertise them and I sold them to people on farms to put in their little ponds.

The first pond I built was way down by the road and it was built after the Forest Service bought the soil for landscaping. When Bob built the lake he built a nice looking dike all around it and it looked real good. Let's go back to building. When I had it dug out there was no water in it, just a great big two acre bowl and I noticed there were a lot of water lizards in there. Someone told me that they might eat the little trout.

My grandson, Victor, who was about six years old, was there and I said, "Victor, you take a bucket out there and for every one of those little salamanders you find I'll pay you a nickel." So he went out and collected all the salamanders. He must have had that bucket full – about one hundred of them. In the meantime someone else told me that the information was wrong and that salamanders didn't kill fish nor eat them. So when Victor brought them in I paid him and then I said, "Now, Victor, take them back and dump them back in the pond." He looked at me with a big question mark in his eyes as if to say, "Grandpa, you must be crazy!" So I had to explain to him why I did it.

After I advertised the fish and got orders for them I built a little fish tank for the back of my pickup and I'd haul little trout that they call "flies" to fish farmers. I bought a pump to keep the water circulating in the tank. When the fish farm was going good I sold lots of fish to farmers all over the country. I'd even haul them up to Ferndale, Blaine, Sumas – all over. They would order maybe a thousand or five thousand of the little fingerlings and I'd deliver them in the tank.

I did a lot of that and really enjoyed it. I even shipped some out by plane over to the lakes. I'd charge $40 or $50 per thousand and sell maybe four or five thousand to a farmer. I'd save maybe ten or fifteen thousand and put them in what they call a little rearing pond by the barn. I'd raise them up to about four or five inches and then I'd throw them into the lake and I went on that way until about 1980.

When I bought that place it had two old houses on it. One was very old and almost dilapidated. It would have been smart to have had Bob take his Cat and smash it down, but I couldn't because we had to have a place to live. So I took a skill saw and ripped open all the walls in it. I put new wiring inside (it was built around 1900), new walls on it, a new foundation under it, new siding, new floors and put a new roof on it. I practically rebuilt that whole house and it cost me about $5,000. We lived there for awhile.

Out in front of the building facing the lake was a shed that they had used for cutting shakes and it was nothing but a shell. I put a cement foundation under it and built another nice little house in there.

I now had two little houses and we moved from the one house into the little house on the lake. I had sliding glass doors to go out in front and overlook the lake and Marie thought that it was the most beautiful spot there was. I was still working for the Forest Service then and building the hatchery at the same time.

In 1970, about a year after I got started on the hatchery, I had to go to a fire over on the east side as I was still working for the Forest Service. Bob had his Cat there so I could rebuild the lake and so I drew a diagram of what was to be done, making it about another half an acre or so larger and taking the dirt and pushing it up on the dike. Bob had made kind of a dike around the lake and filled it in, which worked out real nice. By the time I got back he had it all graded out and he asked me if he had done it right. He had done a perfect job. He was one of the best Cat skinners for doing something like that that I have ever known. He could really do a good job.

So now I had the lake and I got a permit from the Game Department to plant about a thousand trout in it. Of course before that I had to get water rights on the lake, I had to get permits from the Federal Government, from the Soil Department, etc. Anyway, the fish farm looked real good and was profitable. We enjoyed living there very much.

One day a friend of mine came up in his motor home and as he sat out in front by the lake fishing he said, "Jimmy, if you'd put in a pedestal there, I could come up and camp and pay you for it." So I thought about it for awhile and will tell about the trailer court later.

Chapter XXV

Marie and I took quite a few trips during the time I was building the fish farm because I didn't have the trailer park and fish farming was periodic – just a certain period through the summer when I could sell fish. I would hatch out 35,000 to 75,000 eggs. I would advertise and sell the little ones to other fish farmers, so I had quite a busy time. Now I'll tell you about a few trips that Marie and I took.

Marie's mother always said she would like to take a trip over Cascade Pass and down into Lake Chelan but she got too old for that so she wanted Marie to take the trip. One day while we were still living on Montague Street, I came home and Marie had all the stuff out, ready to put in our packs and go on a hike.

I must have been about fifty five years old then and she wanted to go over Cascade Pass, down into Stehekin and on to Lake Chelan. So we got our packs ready and in the fall of the year, probably early September, we drove up to the end of the Cascade Highway. At that time there was no new road over it at all. We just drove right up to the trail head at the pass and from there it was about two and a half miles to hike up to the pass. We hiked up over the pass and had a long way to go down the Stehekin Valley. We went down into the valley and there was an old sheep road from there down to Lake Chelan that we hiked on for about eight or nine miles.

We stopped at a Forest Service cabin there for which I happened to have a key. We stayed there one night and we hiked on down pretty close to the Lake. The lady who ran the motel at the north end of the lake picked us up and took us on in to the motel where we were going to stay. We stayed there that night and then we took a boat trip up the lake. The next day the boat, the "Queen of the Lake", came along and took us on up to the town of Chelan. Our son-in-law and our daughter, Laura Jean, came and took us home.

That was quite a trip and I have some beautiful slides of the country back in there where the maples and other trees were just turning color. They started turning yellow at the bottom and by the time they got to the top they were red. It was a beautiful sight.

About 1976 I was still working for the Forest Service and working on my fish pond too, which I dearly loved to do. I was getting awfully anxious to get out of the Forest Service. I had my time in – my thirty years with them. One day while I was at the lake, Marie came out and said, "Jimmy, why don't you just go down there and tell them you're retiring?" So I thought about it for a while because there wouldn't be much money coming in if I retired. But I retired from the Forest Service, and after that Marie and I did a lot of traveling.

That was one of the best times of our lives. We traveled all over and enjoyed it very much. I took all my annual leave that I had saved up and Marie and I went to Arizona. That was the first year we ever spent in Arizona. We stayed there quite a while. We went to Reno and all around and just enjoyed life. I had locked the gate on the fish farm so that no one would be fishing in there.

We took a trip to Desert Hot Springs and we went to Yellowstone one winter. Marie and I enjoyed that very much. I had bought a good truck and a camper from a person at Whitehorse. One time we took a trip down into the Grand Canyon because we had always wanted to go down there. When I was about sixty-three years old we made reservations to go down in the canyon and stay at what they called the Phantom Ranch. We both took packs and read up on what we were supposed to have. We hiked down there with our water canteens.

We stayed at a motel at the top one night and then the next day started hiking down to the ranch. We were hiking down through the canyon and we got near the bottom. I had always been a good hiker and never paid much attention to my water. I never seemed to notice not drinking it or not paying attention to Marie. I was ahead of her and it was a very warm day. We got down about ten and a half miles. Marie got sick and was about to faint and it worried me. I had asked myself before if I was doing the right thing taking her down there at our age. It seemed like the good Lord said that if He hadn't wanted us to get this far that he wouldn't have let us get this far – so we went down there and Marie got faint and it worried me to death.

We sat down and while we were sitting there in that place that seemed miles from nowhere, along came a gentleman I had never seen before. He was an unusual looking person – tall, copper faced, probably in his fifty's, and he seemed to have come out of nowhere. He shook his finger at me and said, "You have not been drinking your water. In this country the air is dry and it just takes all the moisture out of your skin and the first thing you know you are dehydrated and die."

He said, "Now you sit right down there and you drink that water and I am going to stay here until she drinks enough water to get her strength back. It was a good thing I came by at this time because there are a lot of greenhorns that come down here and they don't know enough to drink the water, whether it is warm or not." He gave me a good scolding and said, "You have been hiking ahead of her and you've been hiking too fast. Now you are a mile and a half from the ranch so you just take your time."

At that time I knew there was a God and that he was an Angel sent from above. I asked him where he came from and he said, "I come from up the trail somewhere." I knew right then that the Lord was taking care of us for we would have died, or Marie would have, if he hadn't come along and saved us.

We went on down the Grand Canyon to the Phantom Ranch. We were supposed to stay there one night, but one night wasn't enough of a rest. We met some people there, very nice people, and they could see that we were older and tired. He was a photographer and they let us have their room for the next night. They were very kind people and we appreciated it. We stayed there for two nights and enjoyed watching nature down in the canyon.

We walked across a bridge that crossed the river and we could watch the rafters coming down the river. We probably saw eighty rafters come by every day. That was quite a thing to take a raft trip down the canyon, on the Colorado River I believe, and it was a long trip. After we stayed there two nights we got up early the next morning and decided to hike out. We filled our canteens and this time we drank the water and we didn't go very fast. It took us all day until seven o'clock that night to get to the top of the canyon. We had a motel room waiting for us. That was one memorable trip down into the Grand Canyon.

That winter I worked around the fish farm.

In 1980 Marie developed breast cancer which scared the daylights out of me. She was operated on and spent a long time in the hospital.

Life slowed down for me because I was really nervous at the time. That was while the road crew was building the highway up here, so we had a good crew in the campground with good people and I didn't have to worry about that too much. I had my daughter, Janet, come in and take over as manager and I stayed with Marie until she got well.

She was operated on in July and that fall I thought that maybe the way things were going we should take some trips while we could. So we got the camper all ready and we were going to take a trip around the United States. We took off and went to Yellowstone and Niagara Falls and we had a wonderful time. Marie wasn't completly well because it takes a long time to get over that kind of an illness. She had been out of the hospital about two months. I had to be very careful not to drive too fast. We enjoyed Niagara Falls a lot.

We crossed over into Canada and traveled on the Canadian side and then crossed back again to the American side. We went on through New York and down through the old Civil War battlefields in Virginia. We spent several days there and it was very interesting. Then we went on to Washington, D.C. and went through the White House and all the historical monuments, the F.B.I. department and other departments. We got a very good education there. Then we went on down to Highway 40 and on our way back we stopped at the Grand Canyon overnight. From there I drove to Calistoga, California where we stayed for a few days.

We spent about six weeks running around and finally made our way back home. After that we did a lot of traveling. That winter we spent two weeks on the big island of Hawaii and the little island. Then we came back home and I spent time at the campground with the campers. In June Marie was feeling really well and we took a bus trip to Disneyland with our friends, Olga and Eddie Woods. That was one of our best trips. We enjoyed that very much and spent a couple of weeks there.

When we came back I had a lot of work to do on both the fish farm and the trailer court together. I figured I had to have help and I asked my daughter, Janet, to act as manager. She and her husband moved in as managers of the place. We ran the place together for two or three years, at which time the road crew moved out and the campground was empty for awhile. We only had one or two campers in there at that time.

To go back on the story, Marie and I wanted to take a trip across the United States so we took off and drove up through Utah, stopping at Salt Lake City for awhile and then went across into Colorado. We got as far as a town called Colorado Springs. There were a lot of Texaco and Shell people there investigating shale rock for oil and they had taken up all the motels. We couldn't find a motel and we had to turn around and come back toward Utah, about fourteen or fifteen miles, before we found a motel. We were lucky. We stayed there that night and Marie said she didn't want to try to go across the United States, she just didn't feel up to it and had other things on her mind.

We came back across the border line and drove to a town called Moab, way up in the southeastern part of the State of Utah. It was a recreational town. We signed up for a trip down the Colorado River on a raft. We stayed there that night and the next day we were taken thirty miles up the river. We had a lady guide. I had a camera and sat in front of the raft so I could get some pictures. Rafting on the Colorado River is pretty well controlled by the State or Federal Government because you are not supposed to be on that river in a raft or a boat without a permit.

While we were getting ready to go, there was a young couple who came down the river in a canoe and our guide said they weren't supposed to be there – that it was against the law. There was a dog sitting in front of the canoe and the man and woman waved to us as if there were nothing wrong. The guide said they were going to be in trouble. The dog was barking something terrible, as if it knew that something was wrong. We waved to them. We let them get ahead of us and then we started down the river.

We got down to a big whirlpool and we heard a dog barking or howling. The guide steered us real close to that whirlpool. The dog was caught in it and I tried to reach down and get hold of him, but I missed him by about two feet. We radioed the raft behind us and they were able to pick up the dog. What happened was that the canoe had tipped over and the dog had fallen out. The man was on one side of the river and the lady on the other and the canoe was plastered up against the bank. When the canoe turned over they had lost all of their equipment.

The guide went over to one side of the river and picked up the woman and then took her over to the side where the man was. They were tickled to death. We could see that they knew they had done wrong because they were so quiet. The guide told them that they had better report to the police station in Moab because what they had done was against the law and they should face the charges. They had lost everything they had.

We went on our way and got to Moab about three-thirty in the afternoon. It was a very enjoyable trip and from there we headed back home.

Chapter XXVI

Between 1977 and 1979 I just worked on the trout farm to improve conditions. In the summer of 1979 I had a friend come up from down below to go fishing. He had a motor home and he stayed there. He was standing on the dike where we were fishing and he said, "Jimmy, if you put in a recreational pedestal here with electricity and water and sewer I would rent it from you and and I could come up to fish." I thought, "Why don't I do that?"

I could get some electrical plugs, etc., and put them in – but first I would have to get a permit from the power company or the State to put in the electricity. I went to the State Department of Industry and they gave me a permit. I knew the inspector, Jack Smith, and I was telling him about my project. He said, "Jimmy, you just don't put a plug in. You have to have a whole camping pedestal that has all that – a special plug – a large plug that has to be a 130. If you put in the wrong kind you're liable to burn up the camper and get yourself in trouble."

I found a place that had three of those special pedestals for putting in a trailer park. I hired a local man to take a backhoe and dig a ditch down one side of the place and over to the barn where I had the big electrical panel put in. I had a ditch dug wide enough for a sewer system and a water system and the electric line. Then along came the television cable, but no telephone yet. I went to the city and got a permit to put in a septic tank. I wasn't sure if I was in the city limits or not. I put in one septic tank and ran sewers for three pedestals. Each pedestal took care of two campers so I had enough room right there for six campers, or rather eight, as I had four pedestals.

I put those in and had the ditch dug a little further. I got them in by 1980 and I no more than got them in when the people started rebuilding the mill. They put in a computerized mill and they began to hire people. The first camper that came in there to rent by the month was the purchasing agent for the mill. He had other people down there who wanted to work and along came electricians and welders and so forth. They all wanted to rent space and I ran out of room. I had ditches dug all down and around and I put in ten more hookups. I had eighteen campers in there so I had to put in another septic tank and I had that campground full. It amazed me how fast that place filled up.

The next thing I knew, the county came to see me because they found out that I had put in a campground. I went to them to get a permit to put one in and they gave me the run around. I couldn't catch up to the right person so I just put one in anyway. Well, along came the county, because the woman next door didn't like the campground and called them. They were going to sue me and fined me $300 for putting in the septic tanks without a permit.

Well, I got on the ball and went down there. They tried to catch up with me and they called me into the courthouse. There were about six of them sitting around there and they were going to tell me this and that but their engineer stopped them. He said, "Listen, he has a permit and it is registered as a campground." When I first made the campground I went to the county and had a name, "Cascade Camloop Trout Farm" designated as recreational area and sure enough I had that, so they couldn't sue me. But they could make trouble for me and they made me put in another septic tank. To make a long story short, I had a lot of trouble with the county fighting that thing through, but finally I had a campground that took care of eighteen trailers.

The first year I had it filled with millworkers. I had them in the campground about two years. I was making pretty good money on that because I think, at that time, I charged them $70/month which was pretty good and that gave them sewer, lights and water. They had to get their own telephone and televison hookups. I had all types of campers, all types of people – some were alcoholics, some were good people – just a general run and you had to be on your toes all the time and watch that they didn't go off and leave without paying.

Anyway, the county gave me a bad time all the while I was building it. Getting water rights was a real hassle. At one time it was all done under the State Department of Hydraulics. They handled all permits for putting in lakes or putting in culverts or anything to do with the creek. Then all at once, after I got that first permit, something happened and the state turned it all over to the State Environmental Agency.

First I'd asked for a permit to run a pipeline from the lake up above to down below and they let it go for a long time. After about two or three years there came a lady from the State Environmental Department. She said she had found some papers where I'd made a request to put in a waterline from the lake down. She wanted to know if I wanted to continue with it. I said yes, I would like to have a permit to put a pipeline from Kirk's Lake down to the house, with about a forty foot drop. So they gave me a permit to put that in and I had two water rights.

I had to get another permit on another creek that came out of Kirk's Lake and turned north into Lost Lake. That creek ran all year 'round, so I got a permit to come from that lake down. While I was putting in the lake there came another department of the state, hydraulics or something, and said I had to have a permit to do anything with the lake. I already had a water rights permit but then I also had to have another permit to work in the lake. It was just permit after permit after permit, but I fought it out and finally got all the permits that I needed.

I got my water lines in and all the little things done. I had a little trouble getting permits to put in water lines around the trailers. I put in water lines all around the campground and I put in the eighteen pedestals. I had telephone and power lines put in and TV cable put in, too. It was finally all done.

We started down to California in September and we got down as far as Grant's Pass. Marie said it was just too hot to continue down there and she didn't want to go, so I turned around and came home. I thought to myself that this would be a good time to build a water wheel. I had had plans to build a water wheel for a long time and I thought this was my chance to do it.

There was a fellow staying in the trailer court who was a computer expert for the mill and he said that if I wanted to build a water wheel he would give me the plans off the computer. I said, "That can't be possible." He said, "You tell me the size of the water wheel you want and I'll show you." So I told him I would like to have an eight foot water wheel. He gave me the plans showing just what size lumber I should use and the very cuts that I would need to make a degree on each side of that water wheel. There would be about six different turns on each side so it would be twelve angles that I had to cut out to make that water wheel.

It's pretty difficult to tell you exactly, but I had to have a real fine saw with fine teeth to cut these out. I bought five gallons of waterproof glue – the best I could get. I started cutting the pattern out and laying it out on the floor in the barn. I glued it and kept working at it until it was complete and it's still up there and running real nice.

I don't know what else I can tell you about the campground. I had it for about thirty years and I worked on it when I retired from the Forest Service. That was my second career and it was a good one. I was very successful in that campground.

It seems as though I never had enough spaces in the campground as there were always people I had to turn away. So I decided to put in an additon to it. I got a permit from the Department of Natural Resources and State Industrial to put in a new wiring system. I put in some new stations and I added about twelve more units to it. After my son-in-law moved out of the old house I burned it down and had the city put in a two-inch waterline. While the ditch was there I added a sewer system and this time I did it right with the county. I got all my permits and nothing went wrong.

I had a son who I thought an awful lot of who had been in the Vietnam War. While there he must have had that Agent Orange sprayed on him because he got cancer and he died that year. That hurt me so very much. I grieved over that so much that I didn't give the campground as much attention as I should have. I could see then that eventually I was going to have to get rid of that campground, as I couldn't justify staying there and fighting the people.

We were getting up in years, Marie and I, in our late seventies. I always thought when I got up around that age I would be able to move around good. My body was good physically but I was hurting and I just did odd and crazy things for no good reason. I stuck with the campground for some time and finally my wife, Marie, couldn't handle all the book work. She said to me one day that after the 7th station she was lost.

Two years after Bobby was gone I finished the other campground that I had started before he passed away. I took in all kinds of campers and I gave favors to people that I shouldn't have. I had a lot of alcoholics in there – about seven or eight of them. I had a real mess there to straighten out and I wanted to sell the place. I got someone to help me and we started moving 'em out of there – the ones who didn't pay –

and I had to start getting rid of the alcoholics.

When you're running a campground you really have to watch out because people will move in and not tell you the whole story. After they get in they will bring in a boy or girl friend or bring in more people. You really have to have a contract with them so you don't get jumped on. That happened and I had to slowly get the idea to sell the campground and move somewhere else because I couldn't put my whole heart into it.

When I still had the trailer court a young mother and her son lived there and they were having a terrible time. They were thousands of miles away from home. The mother thought the world of her little boy and she took care of him and I helped them out a little bit while they were there. She said, "Jimmy, someday you're going to need someone to help you and I'll be there." I just put it off to one side.

Well, the time came when I couldn't see well nor hear well. After Marie passed away I had people helping me. She came and helped me with the housekeeping and drove for me.

Chapter XXVII

In this chapter I'd like to tell about some of my good friends I worked with in the Forest Service.

Jack Swilling came to work for the Forest Service in 1946. I think he had been a welder at Boeing or somewhere down there and had gotten something in his lungs. He told me that he thought it best to be up in the mountains where the air was fresher. He had two sons, Bud and Glen and he had a daughter later on named Vicki. When he came up to Darrington he was in poor health so Harold Engles put him up as a Guard, I believe, at the North Fork.

Jack had a lot of interesting stories. He read a lot. He read the old story of Jesse James and historical books and he was very knowledgeable when it came to the history of our American people or American characters. He asked me one time if I were related to Jesse James because he read a story that there was a James Anderson who was running with the James gang and was caught with a horse that was stolen. They took him to court and were going to hang him, but he pulled a receipt from Jesse James out of his pocket for the horse and showed it to the Judge. Boy!! The Judge just dismissed that case real quick because they didn't want any trouble with Jesse's gang.

One time he told me that in Texas there were around 69 destitute counties that weren't good for anything. Later on he told me that Texas had the largest Forest Service in the United States but there wasn't a tree growing on it. He was very interesting and could tell you all kinds of stories. One day he was helping me cruise timber and he was watching the rear chain for me. I happened to go through a pile of brush and a pheasant flew up and scared the heck out of me. Jack got the biggest kick out of that and said "I bet if that was a bear you'd never stop running" and I said that I probably wouldn't.

Jack was telling me one time about hunting with one of his friends up on the side of Higgins. His friend didn't have a rifle so Jack loaned him one. I believe this is true as to what he told me. They hunted all that day and didn't see a deer. Jack told his friend that he was sure glad they didn't see one because that rifle his friend was using didn't have a firing pin in it. That friend didn't speak to him for a long time.

One time he invited me down to his house for coffee. His wife, Isabelle (he called her "Izzy"), had some favorite coffee cups on the wall that she had collected and I didn't know that. Jack reached up and grabbed one of those cups and poured me some coffee. We were drinking the coffee when Izzy came in and just jumped all over me for using one of her collection items. Jack got a big kick out of getting me into trouble.

Jack was a guard at the North Fork Guard Station for several years and he liked that. He and his family would be up there (that was in 1946 or 1947) and he had a crew of eight or ten young men working for him in the summertime. Art Ryals headed up the Suppression Crew. They would spend the whole summer up there working on trails and roads, planting fish and doing a lot of good work for the Forest Service. They also had a fire crew. I had them up on fires and Art had taken them on fires and they also were on the Chilliwack fire, I believe.

One time Joe Hollingsworth, Art Ryals, Jack Swilling and myself were planting trees up on the side of Gold Hill. It was wintertime and cold and just miserable rain so we were going to build a fire for lunchtime. We found this great big old fir snag that had a lot of loose bark on it and we decided to knock some of that bark down for our fire. Sometimes when those old snags got dry the bark would loosen up way up to the top.

Anyway, Joe took an axe or something and started loosening that bark and all at once all of it came down at the same time, right where we were about ready to build the fire. All of us took off. Joe was way down there anyway – and Jack and myself. I don't know just what position I had – and then there was Art Ryals. Well Jack fell down in the brush and Art just ran over the top of him and on down through the brush. After everything had settled down Jack said "Art, you ran right over the top of me." Art said, "Well, I had to get out of there and you were in my way." It was comical to see one fall down and the other one just run right over the top of him.

Grace Tucker was a famous cook, you might say, for the Forest Service in Darrington. She cooked for the road crews, she cooked for the suppression crews, she cooked for the fire crews, she cooked for the trail crews and all the different crews. Grace was also a member of the Darrington School Board and was very active in that. She had five sons – Tommy, David, Byard, Jim and Harry and one daughter, Carol.

Most of the boys were active in the Forest Service. Tommy was a recon man at the time, reporting for roads; Byard was a trail locater, located new trails and reported what should be done with existing ones; David worked on timber sales. Before Harry went to college he worked in the lookouts many times. Jim was a meteorologist and if he worked for the Forest Service it was before I came. Now Jim and Harry are gone and Mrs. Tucker passed away. She was very well liked by a lot of people. Her husband was one of the first rangers in Darrington. He had a Ranger Station down at Clear Creek in the early 1920's I believe – sometime after World War I – because he was a World War I veteran.

Joe Hollingsworth was born and raised in Oso and was a logger. He must have been about twenty years older than I was. The first time I met him was in 1942 when he came up to French Creek Lookout where I was working. He came to get my Social Security number and fill out some papers for me. He was a very precise person. He had logged all his life and he said he had a weak heart and had to find an easier job than logging.

The second time I worked with Joe was on a trail going up to Prairie Mountain. There used to be a trail going up there and we had to open it up in the springtime for the horses. Joe and I worked on that trail. We took our saws, a crosscut saw, an axe, a wedge and a few other things. When we got up there a ways there was a sizable log across the trail. It must have been three or four feet through. It was turned down on a bank and was up off of the trail quite a little ways. The log was supported on both ends so it sagged in the middle.

Of course, not knowing everything about the woods at the time, I grabbed the crosscut saw and I started to buck at it. Joe turned around and said, "Uh, uh, Jimmy, you're going about it all wrong and I can see that you have not cut many logs out of the trail." I said that was right and he said, "Well, I want to show you something. If you keep on sawing like that you won't get down there very far before that log would pinch the saw and you'd have to chop it out." He said, "Now the best thing to do is to take an axe and slide it underneath the log so that it will ride the saw on the handle and it will saw into the log." Then he showed me how to do it.

It's pretty hard to explain just how it was done but the axe supported the saw while you sawed and you couldn't saw too hard because you'd knock the axe out. We sawed about half way through it, or maybe a little more, and then we took the saw and sawed around the top. Of course, after we sawed down a little ways the log broke in half. Joe taught me something I had never known before. He was a good foreman and an easy fellow to work for. I thought he was a little slow but he was just very precise and did everything just right so that nothing was missed.

I worked with Joe for several years. He was married to a woman named Sylvia, had twin daughters he called "Tippy" and "Toppy" and he had a son named Calvin. At that time, Tippy and Toppy must have been about seven or eight years old, a little older than my daughter, and they were going to school up here. They seemed to be a jolly crew and very religious. Sylvia was very religious and they belonged to, and worked for, the Baptist Church.

Joe worked at the Ranger Station doing jobs that he knew how to do best. He told me a lot of stories. He talked about being a choke setter in the log camp and about working with, or supervising, an Indian named Jimmy Price.

Now it seems that Washington Veneer was logging up here and had about forty acres to log. That was a setting. Now a setting in a log camp could be all the way from fifteen to forty acres. It was where you could reach everything with a cable. They would need a spar tree and my job in the Forest Service was to find the spar trees. Sometimes I'd go out in the middle of the setting and see where I could reach all of it without pulling the logs over a hill or stumps so it would be clear. I would mark it with a cross and the rigging crew foreman would pick out one of the trees that he needed to rig.

There was a high climber who was a professional – very good, very strong and not afraid. He would put on his high climbing boots and go out and saw all the branches off this tree – maybe a hundred feet up. He would put in a little block and pulley and would run the straw line down to the ground. The donkey there would hook on to what they called a "bull block" which was a huge, huge block that weighed four or five hundred pounds. They would ship that up to the high climber then he'd get a cable and wrap it around the tree. He'd wrap that bull block down with cable, nail it down, then he'd send the straw line down, he'd get an inch and a quarter and a half cable and it would be the main line. The main line would be pulled up through the bull block, then down. He had it fixed so that they could move it around the tree and pull the logs up to the spar tree in a cold deck, which is just a big pile of logs, or they'd have a loader to pick up the logs, put them on a truck and haul them down to the mill.

It seems that at the end of a month it was payday and there was going to be a three day holiday. They wanted to get all the logs out and get that one setting all cleared out. Jimmy Price happened to be bucking the last log in that setting and it was a huge one. Joe and his friend were setting chokers. They went down to get the log and Jimmy Price was still bucking it. Joe said, "Hurry up, Jimmy, this is our last log and we want to get paid and go home for our holiday." Jimmy Price was a great big, powerful, husky person and he turned to Joe and said, "You cut."

Joe said he grabbed hold of that saw and he could not move it as it was stuck in the log. No matter how hard he tried he couldn't budge it. Jimmy Price looked at him and laughed and said, "a weak white man, just a weak white man," and he reached down and started bucking on that log. He pulled the cutter off and pulled the log out. Joe passed away at the young age of about fifty-one. He had a weak heart. His children were still young.

Nels Bruseth was a great man in the Forest Service who spent his entire career there. Nels was raised down in the southern part of the state near the bay. He said that when he was little he had a heart disease and he was very thin and not very big, so he decided to come up here to the mountains to get his health back. He came up and worked for the Forest Service, but that was long before my time, probably around 1911 or before, when the Forest Service first started.

He was the first man on Mt. Pugh Lookout. The Forest Service had a lookout on Mt. Pugh and Nels used to man it in the summertime. He had a girl friend who lived down by Bedal. There was a little town down there, a settlement, and his wife-to-be stayed there with her uncle. They were Norwegian and Nels was full-blooded Norwegian. In the evening he would take off from the lookout and run down to see his girlfriend. It was a long way down and a long hike back. That was quite an ordeal and you had to be a powerful person to do that.

There are a few pictures of Nels taken in the lookout back then – years ago. Nels was an individual who was well read about nature. He read a lot of books on botany, etc., and if you picked up a plant he knew exactly what it was and could tell you all about it. When we were working on a trail and would get tired, we'd go and pick up a plant and say, "Nels, what is this?" And he'd say, "Go sit down and I'll tell you all about it."

I'll always remember the time I picked up a little plant that looked like a miniature palm tree. I asked Nels about it and he said, "Well, sit yourself down and I'll tell you all about it." He said it really was a miniature palm tree only about two inches high and it grew on moss floors. He said that millions of years ago, during the Ice Age, the earth made a big turn. The southern part went up to the north and there was a quick change. Everything was frozen. It was the Ice Age and as it thawed everything flowed south in chunks. That was what cut out a lot of our canyons and such. The flows smashed a lot of plants down that had been in the southern part of the world. He was a very interesting person to listen to.

One time up on the side of Higgins there were some blue flowers growing. Nels was always taking pictures and he was also a great painter. He ran across these blue flowers, I forget what he called them, and he had me hold them just right for his photo. He had pictures of all different kinds of flowers. The way he would paint his pictures a lot of times would be to take slides of the subject and put it on the screen, sketch it and then he would paint the picture. I have a couple of his paintings that he did years ago. I have one of Whitehorse and another of Meadow Mountain and I wouldn't trade them for anything.

To go on with the story, Nels was a great painter and he painted in a way you wouldn't understand. He'd take his pencil in the palm of his hand, not like we draw, but take it with his whole hand and draw a picture. One time he had taken some slides up on Meadow Mountain while we were there painting signs at places along the trail so we wouldn't get lost and so other people would be able to find the trail. He got paint on his hand and got it on the camera lens. I said, "Nels, you've got paint on the lens and you'll not be able to take any more pictures." He wiped the paint off his hands and the lens and he did take more pictures. It seemed like everything he did was good.

One time Nels and I and a character named Jimmy Strom were up on the side of Higgins. Jimmy and Nels were very interested in gold mines. Jimmy told Nels that his father had a mining claim about half way up there, so Nels said, "Let's go look at it." It was lunchtime and I said I would stay. They took off and hiked up to that old mining claim and I walked around and found an old shed right close to the trail that they had taken. It was an old horse shed that was used when they logged there for logs to be used for telephone poles. They used a team of horses to pull them out of the brush. The horses stayed in the shed and there was a lot of dried horse manure in there.

I was standing in the shed when I heard Nels and Jimmy coming. Jimmy was partially blind and couldn't see at all without his glasses. I picked up one of those dried horse buns, threw it and hit Jimmy on the side of the head, knocking off his glasses. The horse bun fell on the ground and he picked it up. He was holding it when Nels came along and asked, "Jimmy, what is wrong?" Jimmy said, "Those squirrels are picking cones and one of those cones hit me right on the side of the head." Nels was very observant and he looked around and could see that there were no fir trees around, nor cones. He said, "Let's see the cone." He picked it up and looked at it, smelled it, tasted it and I got to laughing so hard I gave myself up.

Another time Nels was working with us up Clear Creek on a trail. I had a trail crew including Jimmy Strom, Bud Hyatt and his cousin. We were way up there and had three trails to work on. We had the Deer Creek trail that went over to Lake Kelcema, we had the Boulder Creek trail that went up over Deer Pass and down into Verlot and we had the trail that went into what was called, at that time, the Inside Pass. We were stationed there for quite awhile. We called down one morning when it was pouring down rain and we didn't want to go out in it. Jimmy and Bud were still in bed and we hadn't had breakfast. Nels got on the telephone and said, "Jimmy, don't you guys go out in that rain as I am coming up and will be there in a couple hours. You stay there until I get there." So I turned to Jimmy Strom, who was sitting there, and he asked what Nels had said. I told him that Nels said he was coming up to go out with us today and he'd be here in a couple hours and he told us not to hurry off. Jimmy got a big kick out of that because he was in bed anyway and not about to hurry off.

Nels did come up later and helped us work on some of the trails. When he first came up he asked me if there was something to eat and I said that I hadn't started cooking yet, but that I had some rice I'd cooked a couple of days ago. I'd put it in a little kettle, set it up on a shelf and a mouse had gotten into it and that I was going to throw it out. He said, "No, no, I'll eat that" and he threw the mouse droppings one way and took a bite (he was a rough individual), then threw more droppings the other way and took another bite. Jimmy Strom and the crew got a big kick out of that.

Anyway, as we went out we started up to Squire Creek and the last trail we worked on was the Squire Creek trail. We started over Squire Creek Pass and down the other side. When we got up to the top of Squire Creek Pass there was still snow on the ground. What amazed me was that there had been a bear who had come this way and had walked just as straight as a die down the trail. I wondered if we would run across him. Nels was taking a lot of pictures and we had been up there about two weeks and were pretty well worked out.

Nels once told me a fable that the Indians had told him about the mountains. They said that thousands of year ago Whitehorse got into a big fight with Higgins and reached over and scratched her and that is how she got all those markings on her. But the truth is that Higgins is a unique mountain and we don't know whether it pushed up from the earth or if the ocean covered it. We can go up there and find palm trees or palm leaves in the rocks and on this side of it, right below the steep part, if you look for them, you can find fossiis of all kinds – fish, clams and seaworms. Sometimes the University of Washington sends students up to look at the site.

Jimmy Strom was a young fellow at that time in the Forest Service. During the war he had a job down in the shipyards as a typist. His eyes weren't too good and he couldn't see to type without wearing real thick glasses. That was what had kept him from going in the Army and he felt a lot better about coming to work for the Forest Service. He was a nervous type of person who smoked a pipe and the two of us would get into some awful arguments. Anyway, they sent the two of us up Clear Creek one time to repair a telephone line which had been broken somehow and pulled through the insulators. These insulators were a different type than you see now. They were round and had to be wired together to make them work. When you had a broken line you had what they called a sleeve and a crimper. You put both ends of the line together and put them into the sleeve. One fellow would hold them in the sleeve and the other fellow would take the crimper and crimp it so it would hold.

On this particular spot on Clear Creek the line had broken and pulled down over a stump. We thought we could fix it by pulling it together. There was a log running out over the bank and it stuck out quite a litle ways. Now let's go back. Most of those lines were made out of metallic wire. They'd run a No. 9 wire, one wire, and in each telephone you had to have a ground wire that ran into the ground – something to really make the electricity go there. Each phone was a little generator in itself and when you cranked it you pushed electricity right down the telephone line and anybody hanging on to it would get a shock.

Anyway, we got the line up there and Jimmy was going to hold it in the sleeve. There was only room for one at the time on the log so he scooted up ahead of me and he got the line and got it in the sleeve. I got my arms around him with my crimper and started to crimp it and all at once he went sailing out over the brush. What had happened was that Hollingsworth, or someone down at the office, had decided to try to phone Verlot and the line we were working on was between Darrington and Verlot. It went up the Clear Creek trail, over the Boulder trail, and down about twelve miles into Verlot. Jimmy went sailing through the air and he got up and cursed me for pushing him off the log. I hadn't pushed him off but the electricity had shocked him off.

He just had to have something to yell about and we argued for a long time. So he said, "O.K., Jimmy, the next time you get up here and you hold the line and I'll crimp it." So we did it that way. He got up in front of me with the crimpers and I stayed behind and reached around him, got the line together and had just gotten it together before another shock came. I had to let loose of it because it hurt. There are times when you grab the line and get a shock and if you are holding on to another person the juice goes through them, too. That trick had been pulled on us by Nels many times when someone was using the telephone who shouldn't have been handling it.

The most important person to me that I met in the Forest Service was the ranger, Harold Engles. He came about six months after I did. Charles Thurston was the ranger when I was hired and after about six months he left. Harold Engles came up from the ZigZag Ranger Station down at Mount Hood and he was not feeling too well at the time. I met him up at the French Creek Lookout when I was fire watchman at the trail observation tower. Harold Engles was tall, about 6'2", broad shouldered, a copper colored person who weighed about 220 pounds. He was a kind and gentle person and he always rode high in the saddle for me. He was my hero while I was in the Forest Service. I thought the world of him and so did everybody else. He wasn't easy going but he had a heart and was good to everyone. For example, when my little girl got sick and we had to take her to the hospital, he was right there ahead of us to see that everything was O.K. He took care of me like a father and I always thought a lot of him.

I worked with him for about eight years and he'd tell me stories about things he had done when he was a young man and things others had done and so forth. I'll away remember the story he told me about Darrington in about 1910. I don't know if he was here then but a big forest fire started down in the valley just this side of Swede Heaven in what they call the Sand Hill. The timber was around eight to ten inches in diameter, or a little more, and the fire caused it's own draft. Harold said the draft of that fire was so powerful that it would pick up trees nine to ten inches in diameter and carry them away ahead of the fire. It took a long time before they got that fire out and that was about the time Texas Pond burned.

One time Harold went way back in to Cadet Mountain, which is way up toward Bedal. A Boy Scout had fallen over a cliff and been killed. That's about twenty-five miles from here and Harold hiked way back in there, put that young man on his back and carried him out. He was a powerful man and they tell me he was strong enough to bend horseshoes, though I never saw him do it. I wouldn't doubt that he could. He was one of the best hikers the county has ever known outside of Harry Bedal.

Harold always told the story about working on Three Fingers with Harry Bedal. They cleared the top of it and blew off the top of it to make room for a lookout. When they were ready to come home they thought that they would take a short cut instead of coming down the regular Boulder Trail from Three Fingers right over to Darrington. They went over Mount Bullon and down the other side. Harry Bedal was a great hiker and he just showed Harold up. Harold said Harry could out walk him anytime. Harold said he would try to keep up with him but couldn't. He would fall down and stumble and Harry would make some remark about white men who try to hike. He said that was one time that he shut up about being a hiker. Anyone who could make that trip would have to be tough because it's, I don't know how many miles, and it is really rough terrain to go up Bullon, down Bullon and Three Fingers, down by Whitehorse, Buckeye Basin and down through those rocks and brush. It was a tremendous hike.

He also told about the time there was a fire on Higgins. I suppose this story has been told in other books. They had a big fire going and had a fire crew up there. Harold took all the men, and the boss, from the mill at Hazel to fight that fire. He had the authority to take anyone on a fire who was able to go. Mr. Kennedy, the man who owned the mill, was very upset and quite mad about Harold taking all of his men up on that fire. He didn't like Harold and was going to have Harold worked over. So he sent to Seattle and got some kind of a pug fighter to go up on that fire and give Harold a lickin'.

Well, this fellow saw Harold coming down the hill and Harold was wearing this special pack he'd had made for himself from two-by-three's (it had to be extra strong because he carried pumps and other gear in that pack). When this fellow saw Harold coming down through the woods with that pack on and a Bingham pump on it, he asked him who he was. Harold told him and the fellow just came back. He said, "I'm not going to try to tackle a man that's powerful enough to carry a Bingham pump and all that hose on top of it through the woods."

That's just one story about Harold. When you worked for him he expected you to do a good job and work and earn your money. He was very good and I always held him up high.

◆ ◆ ◆

After I came back from my leave and started working for Harold, he had an engineer working for him by the name of John Newman who had been a Major in the Army. He wasn't a loud or boisterous person, but rather gentle and I didn't know whether I'd get along with him or not. He still had some of that military style. Anyway, one day while we were out in the field Harold called and sent us up on the side of Lamson Ridge where there were some switchbacks way up on the hill. For some reason Harold wanted to know the elevation from one switchback up to the other. So he sent John Newman up there to measure it off.

I was John's assistant and went with him wherever he went, to hold the rod, or do whatever he needed. When we got up to the road John said "I don't have a rod with me and it is too late to go back so what are we going to do?" Then he asked, "Jimmy, how tall are you?" I said, "I'm 5' 7½" – 5' 4" right to my eyes." He took his level, had me stand on the ground, and shot the top of my head. Then he'd have me walk up the side of the hill to where he could see my feet and come back up and shoot at the top of my head. We went up step by step. I guess we went up about seventeen Jimmies to the second switchback.

When we got back to the ranger station I thought that Harold Engles would really raise cain. He asked John how far it was from the road up to the switchback and John said, "I think it was seventeen Jimmies." Harold looked at him with a puzzling look and said, "What do you mean, seventeen Jimmies?" They both had a funny sense of humor. John said, "Well, I didn't have the rod with me and it just wasn't worth coming all the way back for it. I figured you just wanted a rough figure on it. I took a shot at Jimmy's feet and at his head and it was seventeen Jimmies up there. I figured he was five and a half feet long and I multiplied by seventeen and that's your distance from one road to the other." Harold got a big kick out of that because he never did believe in exact perfection anyway. What he wanted was a good job. When John read this he said, "Jimmy should have been glad that I wasn't taking horizontal measurements."

One time I was helping John survey from one corner to another, and as you know, there are 5,280 feet in a mile and 2,640 feet in half a mile. Anyway, he had me chaining down the hill and I was reading the tape which is a 200 foot chain you might say. As we came down the

141

hill I'd stop at stations that he had marked and I would read him what it said and he'd measure it. One time when we got down to the end of the road, down to the quarter corner which was supposed to be 2,640 feet approximately, he couldn't find 33 feet in that chain. He just couldn't find it so he said, "Jimmy, show me where 66 feet is on the chain." I had been reading that chain upside down and instead of 66 feet I'd been reading 99 feet.

I thought that I was in trouble because I'd read it upside down. I thought, "Boy, he's really going to chew me out for this," but all he said was, "Jimmy, we've got to go back and measure it again. We did and I thought that was pretty cool of him. I always remembered from then on to look at the head of the chain and the back of the chain – if it's 66 feet then there'd be a 67 on one side and a 65 on the other, and if you were up at 99 feet you'd have a 100 foot difference. If you paid attention to what you were doing you wouldn't make that mistake.

About thirty years ago John started doing some engineering jobs around town. A fellow over here had some property down river and he wanted John to survey it. They had logged it and when they log a piece of land they run a lot of what they call "cat roads" which are little roads going out through the woods to do the logging and take the logs to the landing. There were cat roads all over that property and you could drive over them with a jeep. John Newman picked me up as his chainman and rodman and he did all of his work with a Theodolite. He did this job with an Alidade, which is where he just drew a picture of it, and he was very good at that.

We took our lunches one day and drove down in there, parked the jeep and walked around for about half a day. About noon John said, "Jimmy, you go back to the jeep and get our lunches." So I started back in what I thought was the right direction and got to one place and didn't find the jeep. I walked around some other cat roads and I thought, "It has got to be here somewhere." I walked up one cat road after another looking for that jeep. I must have spent half an hour or so looking and it should have been right there.

I finally heard someone chopping and I wondered what in the world anyone would be chopping in here for. I went over there and it was John clearing some brush. He said, "Jimmy, where are the lunches?" I said, "I can't find your jeep, it's lost." He said, "Well, we'll work a little while and then go find it." So we worked a little while and then we looked and looked and looked and toward the end of the day we found the jeep. It was quite amusing in a way, but costly. We decided that the next time we came there we would tie some ribbons or string and keep tabs on where we parked it.

The land along the river is pretty well mixed up because when it was logged they left brush, etc., everywhere. This was on the Sauk River, above the bridge, about ten miles from town. Now the highway goes right by it.

❖ ❖ ❖

Verne Hicks was a timber sales officer at the Forest Service years ago. He was a young forester and had quite a sense of humor. He had a wife, a little girl and a little boy. He was kind of an assistant ranger in a sort of a way and he also was one of the first rangers of the Suiattle. The Forest Service made some changes in the boundaries, etc., and made the Suiattle a district of it's own and Verne was the Suiattle ranger. He had a fellow working for him as an assistant at that time by the name of Blackie Burns. I didn't know him very well.

One day Verne was doing something and he got a huge sliver in his finger so he went to Dr.Riddle, who had an office in Darrington at that time. Dr. Riddle was a southerner and he was always whistling. Verne said he looked at the sliver and said, "Wait 'till I get my spud." He went off whistling into another room and out he came with a great big needle – kind of a spud shape – and he dug the sliver out with that big needle. Verne said it was comical in a way because he was whistling all the time. Verne always got a big kick out of that because it was the way Dr. Riddle worked. Dr. Riddle charged $2.50 for an office visit.

❖ ❖ ❖

Bob Mealy was from Foster, Oregon. His folks had quite a bit of timber down there that they logged – "timber barons" you might say. But Bob liked working for the Forest Service. I thought the world of him. He was a wild Irishman and he pulled some of the dirtiest tricks on you, but there wasn't anything in the world he wouldn't do for you. He alway had a habit of throwing rocks and stirring up bees nests and then running, because I was the rear chainman and had to come through behind him. He'd get a big kick out of that. I had a lot of friends in the Forest Service and I liked working there because it was more of a family deal in those days, all the way through.

143

◈ ◈ ◈

Art Ryals was one of the people who came back to work for the Forest Service after I came there in 1942. I was here in 1941 and then came back in 1942 and worked steady in the lookout. Art Ryals had worked for the Forest Service and left about the time I went to work so I had not met him. He worked for Ranger Thurston for awhile and then joined the Merchant Marines. He was in the war for three or four years and then returned to Darrington and went back to work for the Forest Service.

Harold Engles was the ranger then and was a new man to him. Art was a pretty powerful young fellow who handled the suppression crew at the North Fork Guard Station, a crew of about ten men all around eighteen years old. He worked on the trails and cleaned out streams and all that type of thing. The suppression crew was called that because when there was a fire they were the first to go and put it out. Art handled that crew for a long time. I remember that Harold gave him a job, and a very particular job it was, too. He had to blast and cut rock on a new trail up on Mt. Pugh. He did a real good job there and worked off and on for the Forest Service in a lot of different jobs. He is still around and comes to see me once in awhile. He is the youngest of the old timers.

◈ ◈ ◈

I want to mention some of the people who worked in our supervisor's office in Bellingham. Phil Bradner was the supervisor when we had the Chilliwack fire. Another supervisor was Harold Criswell who had an assistant named Newt Field for awhile. Hubert Wilson was there in 1942 up until 1950. Newt Field was the engineer for the Forest Service and he was there until about 1950. All of them were good people who kept the Forest Service in good shape – old timers. After they left things began to change.

I want to tell you a little story that I used to tell Janet and Eleanor when they were real small and we lived in the lookout and they'd be crying or something. It was a story about a family of goats who lived on the side of Three Fingers. There was "Billy" the father, "Nanny" the mother and the "Kid".

One day the little kid said to her father and mother, "Let's just wander away and go somewhere else and see what the other worlds are like." So they took off and wandered, eating their way along until they were over on the north side of Whitehorse and they could look down and see the town of Darrington. The little kid turned to her mother and asked, "What is that down there?" Her mother said, "That is where all those creatures live that you have seen up on the mountain once in awhile. That's where they are all congregated. Some of them are pretty wicked."

"Then the little kid asked, "What is that big yellow animal doing that's going down that road?" Nanny said, "That's a big animal that has legs that go around and all those little creatures crawl into the sides of it's hips. They ride and ride and stop at different places where the creatures live. It takes them all to that one big place each morning and then later it takes them all back to the places where they live."

The little kid said, "Could we dare wander down there?" and her mother said, "No way, there's some of those creatures there who have long sticks and somehow they make fire come out of the end of them. They point it at you and if the fire comes out and hits you it kills you." And she said, "Some of them are wicked and kill us goats and then they take and cut our heads off, put us on a board and hang us up inside the places where they live."

The little kid said, "How cruel and terrible things are." The mother said, "Don't ever wander down there because, although some of them are good, there are some who are bad. Those little places with tops on

145

them are where they live. There are a lot of them down there and more of them than there are of us, so don't go down there. If any of those creatures ever come up here towards you, go and hide in the brush or get in under the trees where they can't see you and they won't go after you. Don't show yourself to them. Most of the creatures who come up on Three Fingers are nice and don't bother us."

Chapter XXIX

After I retired from the trout farm and trailer court I had a house built across from the Methodist Church and it is a beautiful place. It so happened that Marie passed away January 7, 1996 and it hit me hard and was almost unbearable to take. Marie didn't get to live in our new house but one year. I feel lost in it and am sorry now that I ever built it

When Marie and I were married, 59 years ago, we enjoyed one another very, very much and were very close. Marie was a very soft person who never raised her voice or became mad or upset. She loved everybody and never could say a bad word about anyone. She just couldn't lie because I'd asked her to lie for me before and it just couldn't be done

We used to do a lot of traveling and she would ride beside me for miles and miles and never say anything. I would say something to her and ask if she were worried or anything and she would say she was just contented. I believe God just sent her down to me to take care of and sent her to me for a wife. I didn't really realize it until afterward that she was an angel – really an angel.

She was a great musician and her whole life was wrapped up in the Methodist Church and music. That was her whole life and she cried once because she couldn't be with the women at the church. I've seen her shed tears a couple of times. Once when I was going to kick some worthless person out of the campground she cried because the person had some children to take care of. She was that way – just a lovely person – and it nearly broke my heart to lose her. I might have hurt her a few times. I don't know if I did, but I'm paying for it now. I loved her so much and it will be very hard to get over it, but I feel I have to finish this book before I get to where I can't remember anything.

Our last trip together was down to Calistoga in California. That was our favorite place we always enjoyed going. It was such a nice place with a hideaway campground and lots of swimming pools – just like Hawaii to us. The last time we went down there was in November of 1995 and we stayed in Calistoga for two or three days, It was the most wonderful vacation we ever had. We had lots of loving and we loved and cared for each other so I had no idea that this would happen. Had I known in time and watched her, I believe I could have saved her if I had made her take her medicine. Marie told Dr. Shillhammer that she didn't need it, that she was healthy enough. She walked a mile a day and felt fit – but that wasn't true.

I just can't say enough about Marie and I hope to be with her before too many years.

Chapter XXX

As I step out on my front porch I'm looking right at North Mountain and there is a lookout there that was put there back in about 1957. It was put in by helicopter and it was used for awhile but now all they use it for is a radio relay station for Bellingham and different places.

If I look to my left I am looking up the Stillaguamish Valley and I am looking at the North Fork of the Stillaguamish River, the South Fork of the North Fork of the Stillaguamish River and looking at Lamson Ridge. Next to Lamson Ridge is Round Mountain and I am looking right down on Higgins. I can see Higgins from here and right down into the valley. I come back and look to the northeast of me and I'm looking way back into Illabot Peak and Sauk Mountain and some other mountains back in there. Just over the hill is Prairie Mountain, but I can't quite see it.

Whitehorse Mountain

Whitehorse Store

Then to my right is Gold Hill. Gold Hill has had some mining done on it and they just got through doing some helicopter logging there. They logged off quite a bit of it so they will have to let it grow back. That is what I can see from here. Looking back to Sauk Mountain, the Suiattle is down that way and I have covered it all, though I can see part of the ridge on Whitehorse from the front porch. If I step out on my back deck I can see Whitehorse and Whitehorse Ridge right in front of me and the valley and creek that comes down called Squire Creek

I can see Bedal Peak and Gold Hill and all the different mountains. I can see clear up as far as Bedal and Sloan's Peak and right between Helena Ridge and Jumbo is Clear Creek. Jumbo is right south of me and Gold Hill is east of the house. I can see ridges on all of these and can look up to Buckeye Basin on Whitehorse and know that just over Buckeye Basin is Mount Bullon. Three Fingers is beyond that and I can still look way down and see Boulder Ridge down beside Whitehorse.

I can't tell you enough about these mountains. My place in Darrington is situated where I can see better than most people. I picked this site years ago and was fortunate enough to be able to buy it and I can see everywhere from here.

I have came to the end of my stories. They are all true except the story I told the girls about the goats. They are all about what happened around Bellingham and the Forest Service in Darrington and about my good times and bad times working and living amid the beautiful natural resources that were given to us by God.

INDEX

C

D

E

F

G

H

I

J

K

L

M

N

O

Osborn, Harry

P

Peek-a-Boo Ridge 67, 68
Phantom Ranch 120, 121
Plasco, Jim 40, 42
Prairie Mtn. 99, 132, 149
Price, Jimmy 133, 134
Pugh, Mtn. 70, 134, 144

R

Rapid Creek 30
Riddle, Dr. 143
Robinson, Walt 87, 91
Roosevelt, F.D. 37
Round Mtn. 99, 149
Ryals, Art 87, 131, 144
Ryals, Danny 105

S

Samish Lake 7
Sauk Mtn. 149, 150
Sauk River 29, 96, 97, 143
Sauk River Logging Co. 44, 87, 96
Sedro-Woolley, WA 15, 16, 17
Shannon, Gil Dr. 37
Shillhammer, Gary Dr. 148
Silver Lake Scout Camp 24
Skagit River 97
Skykomish, WA 18
Squire Creek 71, 137, 150
Squire Creek Lookout 72, 137
St. Joseph Hospital 34, 37
Stickney, Don 27
Stillaguamish River 29, 82, 99, 112, 149
Strom, Jimmy 136, 137

Wildcat Cove 13
Woods, Eddie 122
Woods, Olga 122
Workman, Mrs. 8
World War I 7, 97, 132
WPA 22

Y

Yellowstone Ntl. Park 84, 120, 122